THE HEART of DAVID JOURNAL

Leading with Vision, Passion, and Wisdom.

VOLUME 9

by David Mayorga

Published by

SHABAR PUBLICATIONS
McALLEN, TEXAS

Most Shabar Publications products are available at special quantity discounts for bulk purchase for sales promotions, fund-raising and educational needs. For details, write Shabar Publications at mayorga1126@gmail.com.

The Heart of David Journal Volume 9
Leading with Vision, Passion, and Wisdom
by David Mayorga

Published by Shabar Publications
3833 N. Taylor Rd.
Palmhurst, Texas 78573
www.shabarpublications.com

This book or parts thereof may not be reproduced in any form, stored in a retrieval system, or transmitted in any form by any means - electronic, mechanical, photocopy, recording, or otherwise - without prior written permission of the publisher, except as provided by United States of America copyright law.

Unless otherwise noted, all Scripture quotations are from the New Kings James Version of the Bible. Copyright@1979, 1980, 1982 by Thomas Nelson, Inc., publishers. Used by permission.

Copyright @ 2025 by David Mayorga
All rights reserved

ISBN: 978-1-955433-35-8

Contents

Preface 6

Chapter 1: Tylenol Prayer! 7

Chapter 2: The Art of Holding God's Hand! 10

Chapter 3: Trusting the Process of Deliverance! 14

Chapter 4: Revival Begins with Confrontation from God! 18

Chapter 5: God's Greatest Interest! 23

Chapter 6: It's Time to Replenish! 26

Chapter 7: Did Judas Iscariot Have Disciples? 29

Chapter 8: The Time When Jesus Was Everything! Part 1 33

Chapter 9: The Time When Jesus Was Everything! Part 2 37

Chapter 10: Stop Trying to be Somebody Else! 41

Chapter 11: It's Time to Graduate from Kindergarten! 46

Chapter 12: What Voice Has Our Attention? 51

Chapter 13: Enabled! 55

Chapter 14: The Few! 58

Chapter 15: Going Outside the Camp! 63

Chapter 16: Time to Watch! 67

Chapter 17: It's Time to Examine Ourselves! 70

Chapter 18: The One and Only Key to Overcoming Fear! 74

Chapter 19: Creator of a Clean Heart - Part 1 79

Chapter 20: Creator of a Clean Heart - Part 2 82

Chapter 21: Creator of a Clean Heart - Part 3 85

Chapter 22: Two Reports! 89

Chapter 23: Though I Walk through 92

Chapter 24: Get Out of the House! - Part 1 96

Chapter 25: Get Out of the House! - Part 2 100

Chapter 26: In Entering the New! 103

Chapter 27: Roots! 108

Chapter 28: Overcoming Darkness! 111

Chapter 29: Living Under the Promise! 115

Chapter 30: Jesus, the Glory of God! 118

Chapter 31: Recognizing the Glory of God! 122

Chapter 32: Contact with the Glory of God! 125

Chapter 33: Transformed by His Voice! 129

Chapter 34: The Beauty of Hearing God's Voice! 133

Chapter 35: The Devil's Schemes! 138

Chapter 36: Making Lasting, Life-Changing,
          God-Pleasing Changes! 142

Chapter 37: Leadership for Our New Season! 145

Chapter 38: Longing to See Who Jesus Is! 148

Chapter 39: The Cost of Advancing! 152

Chapter 40: Cultural Christianity! 157

Chapter 41: From God's Persepective! - Part 1 161

Chapter 42: From God's Persepective! - Part 2 165

Chapter 43: When God Tests the Promise! 169

Chapter 44: Why Has the Lord Defeated Us Today? - Part 1 175

Chapter 45: Why Has the Lord Defeated Us Today? - Part 2 179

Chapter 46: Why Has the Lord Defeated Us Today? - Part 3 182

Chapter 47: The Discipline of *Early*! 185

Chapter 48: The Religious Spirit! - Part 1 189

Chapter 49: The Religious Spirit! - Part 2 193

Chapter 50: How Will I Serve Him? 197

Chapter 51: Have I Lost My Passion for Jesus? 200

Chapter 52: Called to be An Expression of His Nature! 203

For More Books 206

Preface

On the journey with God, people can find many reasons not to follow or even lie to themselves, saying, "Well, God didn't call me to be a preacher or an evangelist to the nations, so why should my commitment to the Lord be more intense or show greater dedication to God's work?" I've met many believers who live half-hearted lives for God. They don't think twice about picking up a drink and getting drunk, even. As far as they are concerned, they are under grace, and it's perfectly okay to have fun. No divine fire in their bones means hellfire in their lives!

It is this kind of mindset that has nearly stripped the church of its power in testimony. Pastors and church leaders do everything but pray! They may have a busy ministry full of good works, but it's powerless! They have spent their time ministering to people, but not to Jesus! Thus, the powerlessness.

Is this truly what it means to live with eternity in the heart? Is this what Jesus died for? As leaders of God's church, we must assess what we, as pastors, leaders, and servants, are communicating to the people. Are these messages emphasizing the salvation power of Jesus? Do they embrace the brokenhearted? Is our ministry training and equipping God's saints for the work of ministry? Whatever God has called us to do, we need to get to it.

The hour is growing late, and the time to stop playing religious games is ever upon us. It is time to seek the Lord in prayer and fasting—this new generation is crying out for something real—they are calling out, **"We would see Jesus!"**

My heart has been longing for the church to return to the place of prayer, fasting, and brokenness! Jesus said, **"For I have come down from heaven, not to do My own will, but the will of Him who sent Me."** (John 6:38) This is not just a great idea, but it is the *only* idea! It's time to embrace His heart, mind, and plan!

- Rev. David Mayorga, *Author*

1

Tylenol Prayers!

"Now this is the confidence that we have in Him, that if we ask anything according to His will, He hears us. And if we know that He hears us, whatever we ask, we know that we have the petitions that we have asked of Him." (1 John 5:14, 15)

Let us begin our devotion today with a comforting truth: When initiated and guided by the Spirit, our prayer will hold immense power with God!

I have discovered that having a prophetic picture of what God has for your life, family, vocation, or ministry makes personal praying more effective and efficient. When servants of the Lord are in tune with God's vision for their lives, their prayer becomes focused and intensified.

When there is no vision for life, when the believer is clueless about what to do with their life, they tend to become relaxed. There is no push to seek God, thus making that believer stagnant in all areas of life.

I have always believed that lazy people weren't born that way; they are lazy simply because they are visionless. If there is one thing that the Spirit of the Lord does in us, that precious Fire of God, it invigorates our earthly nature. It awakens us to follow hard after God!

Personal prayer has a transformative power that few things can match. It brings us into God's presence and opens a direct line of communication with Him.

Regardless of our emotional, mental, or spiritual state, personal prayer has the potential to uplift, heal, and strengthen us.

Be Specific!

One of the most remarkable privileges of personal prayer is the freedom to be specific with God. This is not a mere allowance but a divine invitation to pour out our hearts, expressing our deepest needs, desires, and concerns. What a privilege, indeed!

In this private time with God, one can come clean before the Lord by expressing our fears and fleshly or carnal tendencies. It is also the place where one can confess all sins and failures. Yes, it is where one can make peace with the Lord and find joy and freedom in the Holy Spirit for the spirit of heaviness! There is no place like it in the whole world.

The more specific you can be with God, the more freedom you will receive. The more you retain, the less freedom you enter. So, we must learn to be specific with all our needs before Him. It is at this place where you will find personal deliverance. No demon in hell can stop you from touching the hem of His garment.

Why Pray?

While discussing personal prayer and its value for all believers, I have encountered too many believers who don't have a personal prayer life. It almost seems that some believers don't feel the need to pray or don't see the value in practicing daily communion with God.

Meeting God for a season of prayer is perhaps the best all-around medicine for the spiritual man. Prayer is the method that will make a difference for anyone who practices it.

Too often, these believers need the most help emotionally, spiritually, financially, and even physically.

Somehow, the church has failed to teach the believer the value of personal prayer. Instead of creating people who depend on God, they have the believer depend upon a system, a pastor, and the idea that quick prayers will fix their life's woes. I'm not saying that God can't heal or deliver a person through someone else's prayer, but that man must be taught that God has enabled him to walk in His divine power!

Give Me a Quick Fix!

I have also noticed that many people come to prayer meetings looking for what I call a Tylenol prayer. You know what I am talking about. It's the person who is hurting so much and facing severe issues and comes to the prayer line to receive prayer. His hope is in that prayer.

Whether the man or woman receives from the Lord depends on their faith, but if they do receive healing or a word from God, they are still liable for walking in obedience to God's Word. A prayer doesn't guarantee a one-time fix-all, just like a Tylenol is not a fix-all.

Sometimes, we try to fix cancer with aspirin. We all know that sounds foolish, but these thoughts are bound in the hearts of spiritually immature people. This is where many believers are today, and by many, I'm not exaggerating. People are looking for quick fixes to their life issues and become dependent upon Tylenol prayers until those prayers no longer work.

My dear ones, I believe God is calling us, His church leaders, to a life of discipleship and discipline. Look all around you; the day is far spent. It is now or never! Neh'enah.

2

The Art of Holding God's Hand!

"Then it came to pass when Pharaoh had let the people go, that God did not lead them by way of the land of the Philistines, although that was near; for God said, "Lest perhaps the people change their minds when they see war and return to Egypt." So, God led the people around by way of the wilderness of the Red Sea." (Exodus 13:17, 18)

Have you ever questioned God's sovereignty? Have you ever wondered why God would allow certain things to occur in your situation? What about when you find yourself under challenging circumstances and wonder why God is leading you to make a move that seems unorthodox or at least not what you prefer to do?

I can think of countless times in my life experience when I have had to trust God with every move He allowed in my life. It is not how "I" would do it; however, if I follow Christ, I must trust the process.

Regarding the passage above, I believe that, to some degree, the Hebrew children, under Moses' command, were experiencing this very thing I am speaking about.

God Always Knows What He is Doing!

Trusting God with outcomes takes maturity if we ever want to understand His ways!

Often, our flesh makes us wonder if what we are doing, or where we are going, is the right way, the right thing, or the best thing to do in the given case.

Moses had performed incredible signs and wonders in the presence of Pharaoh and shook all of Egypt through God's power. During the last plague, Pharaoh finally consented to let God's children go and worship Jehovah God in the wilderness.

Questionable Moves!

The way God led His children was (to the human understanding and wisdom) not the best of choices. But then again, will we dare question Him?

When dealing with adverse situations, at least to our understanding, we must first and foremost question the Lord humbly with contriteness and ask Him, "Lord, I am Your servant, and I don't understand Your ways. What are you doing with my life, and where are you taking me today? Show me your face and help me to stand in this holy place!"

The Motive Revealed

As God was preparing to move forward with His plan to liberate the children of Israel, He considered some essential things. These things that the Lord was pondering had to do with the future and the cultivation of His people.

Sometimes, we must understand that what God does in us and around us must primarily relate to His purpose and plan. God's works are never about us as much as His good pleasure.

Now let us read about the hidden motive:

"Then it came to pass when Pharaoh had let the people go, that God did not lead them by way of the land of the Philistines, although that was near..."

You see, I am sure the people of God, as they are being led by God's great servant Moses, are wondering why they are being taken through the middle of the Red Sea (which was a more extended way) instead of by way of the land of the Philistines, which happened to be nearer.

When God is working, He is not thinking of your immediate escape or short-term miracle; I believe God is thinking generationally. He allows our character to be tested amid the adversity and pressure of the situation, thus taking us beyond human help.

Listen: If you can find it to escape, why would you need the Lord to help you? If you can escape from danger alone, you can trap yourself again.

When God delivers us, it is usually through His mighty hand, being that you can't do it alone. When you can't escape from something, and God helps you get out, it leaves an indelible mark on you.

Note: Doing things with your human power only produces two specific types of fruits: arrogance and pride, which God hates!

People Quit Too Easily!

"...for God said, "Lest perhaps the people change their minds when they see war and return to Egypt."

I believe that to the degree that you know God is to the degree that you are tested. If God can trust us with an outcome, He will allow the test to go in a specific direction; now, if we need work in a particular area of our life, He will take us according to that need of character-building in us.

God knew His people all too well!

He knew their way of thinking and how they responded to things. Being the wise God, He considered His children and their reaction to a war. He knew that they were not as bold as they thought. God knew their tendency would likely be to return to where they came from, mainly Egypt. Do you see this?

God Knows All Things!

The spiritual exercises God uses to develop our faith can appear fiery and challenging at first.

However, brokenness develops as we remain quiet and humble in His presence. We begin to understand that God is leading us and not ourselves, and we begin to see His mighty hand and wisdom displayed as we trot along our difficult path.

Eventually, we arrive at the point where our lives appreciate God's sovereignty and tender loving mercies.

Let us learn the art of holding His hand when facing adversity beyond our comprehension. Let us learn to trust Him with His ways. God is never wrong, never! Neh'enah.

3

Trusting the Process of Deliverance!

"And when Pharaoh drew near, the children of Israel lifted their eyes, and behold, the Egyptians marched after them. So, they were very afraid, and the children of Israel cried out to the LORD. Then they said to Moses, "Because there were no graves in Egypt, have you taken us away to die in the wilderness? Why have you so dealt with us, to bring us up out of Egypt? Is this not the word that we told you in Egypt, saying, 'Let us alone that we may serve the Egyptians'? For it would have been better for us to serve the Egyptians than that we should die in the wilderness." And Moses said to the people, "Do not be afraid. Stand still and see the salvation of the LORD, which He will accomplish for you today. For the Egyptians whom you see today, you shall see again no more forever. The LORD will fight for you, and you shall hold your peace." (Exodus 14:10-14)

Excited about Being Delivered! (Exodus 4:27-31)

When I pondered my time with God this morning, I felt like studying these verses. I learned something by asking the Holy Spirit to illuminate the Hebrew children's breakout from Egypt. Allow me to share a few thoughts:

When ministering to people in need, the compulsion, breaking, and pain on their faces and, even more profoundly, in their hearts are apparent.

It doesn't take a rocket scientist to know that someone is desperate for a breakthrough and is crying out for help.

Now, some people cry louder than others.

Some hurt emotionally, others hurt spiritually, some physically, and others have a bit of everything.

I believe this was the case for God's children under the bondage of Pharaoh. They were crying out due to the abuse coming from the Egyptian leadership.

I am sure you have read the story: The people cried out to God for deliverance, and God answered by sending Moses as a deliverer.

We are beginning the deliverance process, and God is preparing to do marvelous work.

Most people believe that God will come and deliver us from situations by carrying us out and placing us in a luxurious limousine without needing to fight or overcome any obstacles. This couldn't be further from the truth.

As the people heard Aaron and Moses share the burden that God had over them, **"they bowed low and worshiped."**

Not Too Excited Now! (Exodus 5:21)

Part of being delivered has to do with the fight. God has a specific process for delivering His people. Some are delivered immediately, others are delivered "as they go," yet others will be delivered by walking out of the process and learning the lessons that will keep them from ever coming back to the original pit of bondage.

When Moses and Aaron finished talking to the Pharaoh, their confrontation with the Egyptian king worsened. [Read Exodus 5]

People thought that God would wave a magic wand and everything would be fine. This was not the case, for these are rarely the workings of God in our lives.

After the conversation with Pharaoh, he ordered more work to be done by the Hebrew children, so the criticism began on their part; just listen: "May the Lord look upon you and judge you, for you have made us odious in Pharaoh's sight and in the sight of his servants, to put a sword in their hand to kill us." (Exodus 5:21)

In Despair!

It is incredible how one situation can change everything in someone's life. I can also see how human faith falters and fails to uphold what we believe in our hearts.

I was taught many years ago that the only faith a man needs is God's faith. If you don't have it, you must ask God for it in every situation.

It is evident that the present situation tormented the children of Israel, and fear in their hearts was controlling all their emotions.

When in despair, people say many things and speculate about the future. Most thoughts or words are not in God's heart, so the actions following will likely not be God's will. For example: "So, they were very afraid, and the children of Israel cried out to the LORD..."

1. Then they said to Moses, "Because there were no graves in Egypt, have you taken us away to die in the wilderness?"
   When in despair, sarcasm will start coming out from our fearful hearts.

2. "Why have you so dealt with us to bring us up out of Egypt?"
   When in despair, we will begin to question the motives of why God is doing this or that.

3. "Is this not the word that we told you in Egypt, saying, 'Let us alone that we may serve the Egyptians'? For it would have been better for us to serve the Egyptians than that we should die in the wilderness."
When under duress and in despair, we will be challenged in our faith and tempted to return to where we came from. We don't fight for what is ours, so we settle for second best. We will tell God, "We never said 'take us out of here.'"

The Greatest Challenge for the Believer!

As I bring this devotion to a close, we must realize that the most significant challenge for us believers is to stay faithful to God and trust Him with every outcome. Is it easy? Not. The greatest challenge in our lives is what develops our character. Character development is what this is all about, not so much our healing or our miracle.

The counsel that Moses gave these trembling and fearful children of God was, "**Do not be afraid. Stand still and see the salvation of the Lord!**" I guess the next question would be, how do we do this?

Do not be afraid. Stand still and see. This means you go deep into your innermost being and hear what God is saying (not what your natural faculties are saying or what you hear, etc.) during your deliverance. What you hear deep within your spirit, that does! Neh'enah.

4

Revival Begins With a Confrontation from God!

One thing I have concluded concerning spiritual revival in our lives is that every revival will begin or be ignited by face-to-face confrontation with God. Revivals are not brought in by bright individuals mapping out what works in society or what is relevant to our culture.

Though there may be some truth to, and at times helpful, the fact that we have statistics, I believe that the revival God is looking for or trying to bring forth is a spiritual revival, not one based on man's surveys and opinions.

I believe that when God finds a man or woman who is surrendered fully and willing to go above and beyond their present state, He draws them to Himself for a visitation.

I believe this was the case in the life of most of God's servants in ancient times and continues to be God's method in modern times.

A Burning Bush Produces a Burning Heart!

"Now Moses was tending the flock of Jethro his father-in-law, the priest of Midian. And he led the flock to the back of the desert and came to Horeb, the mountain of God. And the Angel of the LORD appeared to him in a flame of fire from the midst of a bush. So, he looked, and behold, the bush was burning with fire, but the bush was not consumed. Then Moses said, "I will now turn aside and see this great sight, why the bush does not burn." So, when the LORD saw that he turned aside to look, God called to him from the midst of the bush and said, "Moses, Moses!" And he said, "Here I am." Then He said, "Do not draw near this place. Take your sandals off your feet, for the place where you stand is holy ground." (Exodus 3:1-5)

A man's heart must be first ignited by holy fire. Only when this occurs in the human vessel does God make a move in society. God must first have His man or woman on holy ground to be filled with divine fire.

God touched Moses as He stepped into the holy ground! Here, Moses received a fresh revelation of God's heart and was set ablaze for the rest of his life. Unless a God encounter ignites a man or woman, every effort done in Jesus' Name will be useless.

What Is a God Encounter?

A God encounter is when the man or woman of God comes in contact face-to-face with the Great I Am!

Advancement can only come through a face-to-face confrontation with God. I'll explain:

As the Lord looks for a vessel that He can use, He will confront that man or woman by revealing their sinful nature to themselves. This is the first step in any form of spiritual advancement in God.

Once the vessel recognizes that it is undone without God, it must make a choice. Either it will surrender its will to the Lord or walk away unchanged!

Unchanged!

"As He was setting out on a journey, a man ran up to Him and knelt before Him, and asked Him, "Good Teacher, what shall I do so that I may inherit eternal life?" But Jesus said to him, "Why do you call Me good? No one is good except God alone. You know the commandments: 'Do not murder, Do not commit adultery, Do not steal, Do not give false testimony, Do not defraud, Honor your father and mother.'" And he said to Him, "Teacher, I have kept all these things from my youth." Looking at him, Jesus showed love to him and said to him, "One thing you lack: go and sell all you possess and give to the poor, and you will have treasure in heaven; and come, follow Me." But he [a]was deeply dismayed by [b]these words, and he went away grieving; for he was one who owned much property. And Jesus, looking around, *said to His disciples, "How hard it will be for those who are wealthy to enter the kingdom of God!" (Mark 10:17-23)

In this story, the rich young ruler encounters Jesus face-to-face. Notice that Jesus didn't come looking for Him; the young man ran up to Him. This makes all the difference in living a life of surrender and yieldedness to God.

In this encounter, the young man had a strong desire and willingness to be a faithful servant of God. He manifested, to some degree, some deep devotion by kneeling before Him, not to mention the keeping of the commands.

Outwardly, everything seemed to be there! No one could blame this rich young man for trying. Yet, the rich young man had no clue what it meant to step into God's life. For starters, he wasn't invited to come and die. This will always make all the difference. When the Lord invites us to come and die, it will be the seal upon someone's life that He is called to be an agent of change.

Unfortunately, the confrontation with Jesus didn't end there. The Lord Jesus pressed into this man's heart and told him straight out, "**One thing you lack: go and sell all you possess and give to the poor, and you will have treasure in heaven; and come, follow Me.**"

The fire of God manifested itself through Jesus' words and burned up this man's sensual dreams. This was enough for the man to make a choice. Though he had a noble heart and even made the gesture of bowing before Christ, he had no intention of letting go of the very thing that had bound him to this earth—his earthly goods and possessions.

A Light from Heaven!

"As he journeyed, he came near Damascus, and suddenly, a light shone around him from heaven. Then he fell to the ground and heard a voice saying to him, "Saul, Saul, why are you persecuting Me?" And he said, "Who are You, Lord?" Then the Lord said, "I am Jesus, whom you are persecuting. It is hard for you to kick against the goads." So, he, trembling and astonished, said, "Lord, what do You want me to do?" (Acts 9:3-6)

Unlike the rich young ruler, Saul is possessed by religious demons and ready to bring the church of Jesus to judgment. With all his hatred for the Way, Saul of Tarsus had no idea what God would do in his life.

While on his journey to destroy the Church of Jesus Christ, he was confronted by a heavenly light—it was God! He had a face-to-face encounter with God!

My friends, let me add that Saul of Tarsus also had to make a choice. He could have rejected all that he was experiencing and gone on his way, or he could have surrendered his life to the voice of Christ.

When Saul recognized the voice of God calling him, he was trembling and astonished and said, **"Lord, what do You want me to do?"**

Do you see the difference when invited to follow God's deeper life? Do you know what God can do when someone is summoned to go higher and surrender fully to the cause of Christ?

You and I will always have the choice to surrender to the Lord. We don't have to surrender anything; we get to surrender everything! Neh'enah.

5

God's Greater Interest!

"Then the kingdom of heaven shall be likened to ten virgins who took their lamps and went out to meet the bridegroom. Now, five of them were wise, and five were foolish. Those who were foolish took their lamps and took no oil with them, but the wise took oil in their vessels with their lamps. But while the bridegroom was delayed, they all slumbered and slept." (Matthew 25:1-5)

In His parable of the end times and the spiritual posture of every believer for His return, Jesus brings an outstanding truth: *the reality of the human vessel.*

It is one thing to say to yourself: I am ready and prepared for His soon return, but it is altogether a different thing to live it out daily. To stay in the faith is no easy matter if one is not found faithful in His Word, prayer, and holiness.

Too often, believers succumb to mediocrity because they compare themselves with others. They see how others are not following Christ in the same way that they are and are quick to judge.

We must learn not to compare ourselves with anyone. 2 Corinthians 10:12 reads, **"We do not dare to classify or compare ourselves with some who commend themselves. When they measure themselves by themselves and compare themselves with themselves, they are not wise."** We can only compare ourselves to Christ our Lord. He is the Patterned Son! He is the Way, the Truth, and the Life!

We compare our hands' work in the light of eternity, meaning, will the works I have done for Christ stand against the Judgment Seat of Christ? When the fire of God finally begins to pour, will everything we did in Jesus' Name stand the fire of a holy God? This is what it means to live by the standard of eternity.

We can all carry lamps, show the world, and say, "Look at me! Look at my lamp!" Who knows? The lamp may be fancy or mediocre; only humanity would judge that, not God. I dare say that God's valid opinion on all who boast of their lamps would be of greater interest! What does God think of me as a servant, not of what my hands have created?

God's Greater Interest

Now, a lamp is a vessel that provides light. As you can see, the lamp represents the *external* while the oil to be put in a lamp represents the *internal*. This would be the substance that makes the fire burn and provides light for the lamp.

What we think of ourselves has little to do with fire. The point would be, is there enough oil for the long haul in our spiritual journey? We can boast of our lamps and how shiny they may appear; others may applaud our outward appearance, but what does God think?

The Wise and Foolish

In the parable above, Jesus compares wise and foolish virgins. The wise were considered wise because they brought enough oil for the lamps and prepared for the long wait.

Now, the foolish ones did the same. They prepared their lamps and brought oil, but more was needed for *the wait*. How would anyone know how much oil one needs for this *wait*? After all, this is the last time anyone has said anything about the length of *the wait*!

The *foolish virgins* remind me of many believers today when hard times come upon them, and their whining begins: *No one told me that it was going to take this long. Or if I had known, I would have been ready!* Yet others would dare say, *if my leaders would have warned me, I would have prepared!* I have heard all this and perhaps even used some in my journey with God. This is why they were foolish – they didn't live for the bridegroom or His wedding; they lived for their interests.

They All Slumbered and Slept!

Scripture takes an interesting turn when it says that the waiting continued long, and both wise and foolish fell asleep.

What this represents to me is that tests and trials come to all. The battle rages upon both (the wise and the foolish). But note: Only those who prepared *internally* (enough oil in the lamp) could enter the wedding.

It is not about how often we fall asleep during the wait but whether we are awake when the **"cry is heard."**

"And at midnight, a cry was heard: 'Behold, the bridegroom is coming; go out to meet him!' Then all those virgins arose and trimmed their lamps. And the foolish said to the wise, 'Give us some of your oil, for our lamps are going out." (Matthew 25:6-8)

Living a life full of Jesus is the goal of all faithful disciples! Nothing less than a committed life to the Spirit of God will do in this generation. Let us ensure that we are not just getting by but continue passionately pursuing His heart until the end! Neh'enah.

6

It's Time to Replenish!

"And you shall command the children of Israel that they bring you pure oil of pressed olives for the light, to cause the lamp to burn continually. In the tabernacle of meeting, outside the veil which is before the Testimony, Aaron and his sons shall tend it from evening until morning before the LORD. It shall be a statute forever to their generations on behalf of the children of Israel." (Exodus 27:20, 21)

While in prayer this morning at my office, I came across this passage that speaks of one specific statute as laid out by God and given to Moses to give to his leadership team of priests – the tending of God's lamp, which should never be put out or quit burning.

As I read and prayed, the Holy Spirit moved in me differently. It almost seemed as if God was saying. *I have a word for those who have ears to hear in the general body of Christ.* So, I don't want to come across as some prophet who pretends to have all the answers or cures for the world's maladies. I believe God speaks prophetically to me and those with an ear to hear and the faith to believe.

Oil for the Lamp!

The command was for the people to bring oil from pressed olives. The oil is in the olive, and unless it is pressed and compressed, the oil will not flow. People who walk with God and know God's ways often understand this language. If there is oil, there will be light; if there is no oil, there will be no light. It's that easy.

I have discovered that most believers tend to be oblivious to the cause of spiritual burning in a person's life. Many think that God comes and sets a man on fire with little to hardly any effort at all. This is not so. By the time God touches a man, there has been a long and deep inner work in this person's life.

Before any supernatural provision comes, there must be a natural surrender of the will, heart, and mind. One must yield himself to Jesus by counting the cost of living a life of total surrender to Jesus.

I know that people who live and are caught up in *blissful joy* have no time to stop and refuel their lamps for continual burning and often run out of oil when it matters! Too frequently, believers cover up their lack of discipline, brokenness, and yieldedness to God by outward actions like serving, singing, clapping, and swaying back and forth to tearjerking worship songs. My friends, these elements are not substitutes for a life of brokenness!

The faithful servant of God must grasp this and understand that God's divine order for spiritual burning is contingent upon a man's surrendered life.

The Pressing Must Come!

Listen now: It was God's design that olives would go through a process of pressing for oil to flow out of them. It was this oil that would be used to provide fuel for the lamps. Trying to be a bright light without oil (anointing) is to fool oneself that God is flowing in and through them. Unless there has been a pressing of olives for oil to flow, there will be no fuel for the fire!

People are mistaking talent for the anointing. As impressive as programs are to many, it is the anointing that brings a sinful man from being a natural reprobate to a supernatural being in God. We must never forget that it is the anointing that breaks the yoke!

Why the Pressing Now?

If suddenly you feel arrested by adversity, a problematic situation, or an overwhelming challenge in your life, I truly believe that God is pressing you for oil. We need oil in our lamps to burn.

Getting replenished is not fun. Most people don't even think that there is such a thing.

My friends, even Jesus, told his disciples to return and replenish. Listen to this: **"Then the apostles gathered to Jesus and told Him all things, both what they had done and what they had taught. And He said to them, "Come aside by yourselves to a deserted place and rest a while." For many were coming and going, and they did not even have time to eat."** (Mark 6:30, 31)

But what does replenish mean? In the Cambridge Dictionary, *replenish* means *to return or make something return to an earlier level or size.*

Are You Being Pressed?

If you feel that you are going through some stuff in your life today, it might be that God sees how you are running out of oil and has allowed some adversity to press and compress you for the sake of oil.

Some may look at their circumstances and conclude that the devil is the culprit of such a painful situation, yet there is a subtle and profound cry within, saying, "It is God, not the devil, bringing you to a higher place in Him."

I heard the Spirit of the Lord whisper to my heart: *David, a new season is arising. You need fresh oil for your lamp; a replenishment is coming! The lamp that will shed light on the coming generation of those who are yet to be born is getting overhauled!* Neh'enah.

7

Did Judas Iscariot Have Disciples?

"Then one of the twelve, called Judas Iscariot, went to the chief priests and said, "What are you willing to give me if I deliver Him to you?" And they counted out to him thirty pieces of silver. So, from that time he sought opportunity to betray Him." (Matthew 26:14-16)

"For what will it profit a man if he gains the whole world and loses his own soul?" (Mark 8:36)

"Then Judas, His betrayer, seeing that He had been condemned, was remorseful and brought back the thirty pieces of silver to the chief priests and elders, saying, "I have sinned by betraying innocent blood." And they said, "What is that to us? You see to it!" Then he threw down the pieces of silver in the temple and departed and went and hanged himself." (Matthew 27:3-5)

When I read the story of Judas Iscariot and how things unfolded for this would have been a great servant of God, it was heartbreaking.

There are many stories in the Bible about people who served God but then lost their trust and confidence in Him and followed other gods. Judas Iscariot's is the worst story.

Chosen!

The Scriptures clearly state how Judas Iscariot joined the twelve disciples; Jesus chose him.

In three years or so, Judas Iscariot was given a ministry; he became the treasurer for Christ's ministry. He was the keeper of the offerings, and Jesus trusted him with this responsibility. I dare say that Judas Iscariot was faithful at first, but then his selfish nature began to ooze out of him and started stealing the offerings. [see John 12:6]

Like every hidden sin in us has a way of growing if not dealt with, Judas' sin begins to take a new form. He started with stealing the offerings, but this wasn't enough. He needed more to satisfy his carnal cravings, so he decided to put Jesus for sale. Sin is selfish, and anything to satisfy the consuming fire of the flesh goes.

I wish this were an isolated case, but it is not. The church of Jesus today is filled with believers following in Judas Iscariot's footsteps.

It's About Giving Your Life Away!

Whole groups, churches, and even movements are disciples of Judas Iscariot. These have come into the King with hidden and selfish motives. They see the church as an institution that benefits their fleshly desires and selfish ambitions, not a training place where they will learn how to give their lives away!

Today, in our churches, a whole generation is breeding *takers*, not *givers*!

They look at the cross of Christ as an offense, not as a place to be altered in their selfish way of living.

Is it any wonder why many churches today are trendy? Trendy is a nice word for the spirit of the world.

Churches are trendy & fleshly today because they appease the flesh; they tickle man's ears and don't promote Christ and the life of brokenness He lived out.

I recently had a pastor visit my office and invite me to an event he was putting on; he also told me that his church was one of the fastest-growing churches in America. Was I supposed to be impressed? What was I supposed to say? Does it matter that he is this or that? Let's say that I was kind to this brother, and all I said was, "Good for you!"

Going Deeper Into the Heart of Judas Iscariot!

As I pondered Judas Iscariot's life, I wondered how many times I had played the fool! Judas played the fool countless times. Open your mind and think with me:

Here's Judas Iscariot, one of the twelve disciples of Jesus. Jesus committed the ministry of the treasury to him, and all along, Judas thinks *no one knows what thief I am, but I am going to steal everything in these money bags!* Thinking that Christ would never find out, he did this. This is a fool in action.

As the sin grew, the demand for more grew. So now he begins to find a way to get more money by betraying Christ. The Scripture says, "And they counted out to him thirty pieces of silver."

Can you picture Judas Iscariot [with his pockets full of silver coins] dressed in fancy clothes, thinking he is *all that and a bag of chips*? Using fleshly schemes, ideas, trickery, cheating, and betrayals, all to get adorned outwardly? This is a portrait of many believers today.

Living out their fleshly dreams without God's approval. Saying God blessed me with this or that when God is not even interested in their endeavors.

These believers claim to be Jesus' disciples but will not forsake their selfish lifestyles. In the church, they appear to be the real deal; however, in private, they are scheming for self-aggrandizement and bigger and better worldly things. This was Judas Iscariot!

This man is trying to gain the whole world but is losing his soul in the process. What a picture of today's so-called Christian believer. May the Lord protect us all from this wicked, selfish spirit that was so alive in Judas Iscariot! Neh'enah.

8

The Time When Jesus Was Everything! – Part 1

I want to emphasize this devotion to how our emotions get wrapped up in something we set our hearts to do, follow, or get. When our emotions are high, we will do anything to accomplish the task at hand; for example, when starting a workout regimen, we buy tennis shoes, exercise gear, weight machines, etc. Often, our emotions dictate our investment.

Now, the opposite is also true. When the emotions are gone, so is the investment. We will not give the time of day on something where our feelings are not engaged.

Have you heard the word honeymoon or a honeymoon period? Everything we receive has a honeymoon period. What is a honeymoon period?

Webster's Dictionary has it as 1) *a period of harmony immediately following marriage* and 2) *a period of unusual harmony, especially following the establishment of a new relationship.*

Is the Honeymoon Over?

In our walk with God, I'm afraid that many have lost their love for Jesus. I don't say it to manipulate your emotions. I say it as a type of spurring or provocation, if you will, to evaluate our present condition.

A Man Called Demas

"Epaphras, my fellow prisoner in Christ Jesus, greets you, as do Mark, Aristarchus, Demas, Luke, my fellow laborers." (Philemon 24)

"...for Demas has forsaken me, having loved this present world, and has departed for Thessalonica..." (2 Timothy 4:10)

Demas was once one of Paul's "fellow workers" in the gospel ministry, along with Mark, Luke, and others. During Paul's first imprisonment in Rome, Demas was also in Rome.

There is also biblical evidence that Demas was with Paul during Paul's second imprisonment in Rome, at least for a while. Then something happened. Demas forsook Paul, abandoned the ministry, and left town. Paul wrote about the sad situation in 2 Timothy 4:10.

The Greek verb in the original implies that Demas had not merely left Paul but had abandoned Paul in a time of need. The apostle was in prison, facing a death sentence, and that's when Demas chose to set sail.

There is nothing like a good set of adversity to divide men from boys and women from girls!

Spiritual Evaluation!

"Examine and test and evaluate your own selves to see whether you are holding to your faith and showing the proper fruits of it. Test and prove yourselves [not Christ]. **Do you not yourselves realize and know** [thoroughly by an ever-increasing experience] **that Jesus Christ is in you—unless you are** [counterfeits] **disapproved on trial and rejected?"** (2 Corinthians 13:5 Amplified Version)

The word *examine* literally means *"to test a thing"* as to assess its value.

In our walk with Jesus, we must always be conscious of our spiritual vitality. As one of my mentors says, *we must always fight for the right way to live!*

Walking with Jesus, one can't fall asleep; we can't afford it. One must live a disciplined life to live for Jesus as a disciple. There are no options for the life of God to flow in us.

If we fail to evaluate our lives before God daily, we might lose the most precious thing we carry within – the presence of Jesus.

If we lose the presence of our Beloved, here's what begins to happen...

We Become Insensitive to the Lord's Wishes.

When something is fresh and vibrant, we become sensitive to it. When our emotions are high, we are on top of things. God doesn't have to tell us to do this or that—we discern His wishes and act upon them. We love what God loves, and we hate what God hates. We weep when He weeps, and we rejoice when He rejoices. Our hearts are entwined with His; we become one with Him!

We Begin to Recreate with Our Hands What We Lose in Our Souls!

It is interesting to see how many people are so educated beyond their level of obedience. They know everything about everything but do nothing! Have you seen some of those brothers?

YouTube videos and podcasts are no substitute for intimacy with God. You may sound smart, but no more alive than the chair we sit on.

When intimacy with God is nonexistent, we try to create what is missing in the anointing with our flesh. The singers sing louder and longer, copying every song under the sun instead of waiting for the Lord to release prophetic songs to them. The preacher hides behind loud sermons, fancy platforms, and continual pads on the back! Believers follow what is good, NOT God!

Finally, a Life of Confusion and Chaos Will Follow.

If you are lost today, nothing will fix it unless you return to Matthew 6:33. Once we read and understand it, we must repent for not putting Him first and following our desires.

What should one do when he is lost and in the dark? Wisdom would say, *"Turn on the light!"*

Unless we meet with God and allow His presence to take residence in us again, we will not have the power to please Him.

As I close these thoughts, let us run to the altar and renew our love for Him. Neh'enah.

9

The Time When Jesus Was Everything! – Part 2

In my last devotion, I began by sharing our emotions' impact on us as humans. If the emotions are high, we are willing to invest and even lay our lives down for the sake of a good thing.

If the emotions are low, we will deal with a negative response. I'm not saying it is always this way, but almost surely, negative emotions make us respond negatively.

Why would anyone invest in a losing business? Why would anyone jump off a cliff knowing that he can't fly?

Negative emotions are usually "downers" and will cause us to shrink back. As I said before, it is easy to get excited about pleasing God when all things are going well, but it is a different emotion and response when things have gone "south" and no longer look favorable.

Peter Meant It!

There was a day when Jesus began recruiting disciples, and off to Galilee, He went. He came to a few of them while they were mending their nets. Listen to the story: "**And Jesus, walking by the Sea of Galilee, saw two brothers, Simon called Peter, and Andrew his brother, casting a net into the sea; for they were fishermen. Then He said to them, "Follow Me, and I will make you fishers of men." They immediately left their nets and followed Him."** (Matthew 4:18-20)

This Scripture allows us to see Peter's desire to please Jesus, and it goes a step further to prove his loyalty by leaving his fishing net immediately.

This wasn't just a lighthearted decision on Peter's part, no sir, he meant every bit of it.

Now, Peter experienced God-given revelation as he followed Jesus. Something in Peter made him follow Jesus. Yes, some of it was emotion, but there was a passion and a desire to know God, to know Jesus!

Flesh and Blood Didn't Reveal It!

"When Jesus came into the region of Caesarea Philippi, He asked His disciples, saying, "Who do men say that I, the Son of Man, am?" So, they said, "Some say John the Baptist, some Elijah, and others Jeremiah or one of the prophets." He said to them, "But who do you say that I am?" Simon Peter answered and said, "You are the Christ, the Son of the living God." Jesus answered and said to him, "Blessed are you, Simon Bar-Jonah, for flesh and blood has not revealed this to you, but My Father who is in heaven." (Matthew 16:13-17)

Peter was being prepared for kingdom advancement, and the Lord was ensuring He knew about it. The Lord recognized Peter's revelatory gift and praised him for it.

Along with Jesus' praise, Peter received the keys to the kingdom of heaven. Keys represent access. Peter was on his way to greatness, and Jesus would ensure he got to the place for which he was created.

Up to this point, Peter's emotions were at an all-time high! He was walking in a different anointing, excited about all the possibilities. Yet, Peter had no way of knowing what indeed awaited him.

Peter's Greatest Enemy!

As I have mentioned, emotions are based on what we see and how we feel about a particular thing or matter. Trusting things created instead of the

Creator is a sure recipe for disaster! Our natural faculties will betray us every single time.

As Christ began to open His heart to what was about to come upon Him, Peter rebuked him for talking so "negatively." Peter reaffirmed his loyalty toward Christ and promised never to leave Jesus' side—no matter what! Some things are easier said than done.

Jesus is Arrested!

"**Then all the disciples forsook Him and fled.**" (Matthew 26:56)

After making promises to Jesus that he would never forsake Him, Peter went back on his words; this proves that many things we say when we are emotionally charged up are not kept when we are down and out!

Peter saw the Lord be arrested. He saw the soldiers take him away. He saw the very words of Jesus come to pass before his eyes.

Now that Peter had lost his opportunity to be a world changer, what else was there to do? He failed Jesus in the most miserable ways; he betrayed the King of Glory!

Since Peter lost the fire of God in his own life, he was warming himself with someone else's fire! "**Now the servants and officers who had made a fire of coals stood there, for it was cold, and they warmed themselves. And Peter stood with them and warmed himself.**" (John 18:18)

Restored!

One question comes to mind: Can the honeymoon period be regained? Can the first love be rekindled? Will the Lord restore us to the point of trusting us again with the keys of the kingdom of heaven? The answer is yes!

Before restoration can come and the love for Jesus starts again, there must first be recognition of failure and true repentance. Listen to the word of the Lord: "**And Peter remembered the word of Jesus who had said to him, "Before the rooster crows, you will deny Me three times." So, he went out and wept bitterly.**" (Matthew 26:75)

The restoration that God does in us doesn't begin unless there is recognition of our sin, our betrayal, or our rebellion.

Once we remember how we have violated the Holy Spirit's instruction, we will weep! Then repentance can come, and an awakened life will be the result without a doubt. Neh'enah.

10

Stop Trying to Be Somebody Else!

"So, Saul clothed David with his armor, and he put a bronze helmet on his head; he also clothed him with a coat of mail. David fastened his sword to his armor and tried to walk, for he had not tested them. And David said to Saul, "I cannot walk with these, for I have not tested them." So David took them off. Then he took his staff in his hand; and he chose for himself five smooth stones from the brook, and put them in a shepherd's bag, in a pouch which he had, and his sling was in his hand. And he drew near to the Philistine. So the Philistine came, and began drawing near to David, and the man who bore the shield went before him. And when the Philistine looked about and saw David, he disdained him; for he was only a youth, ruddy and good-looking. So the Philistine said to David, "Am I a dog, that you come to me with sticks?" And the Philistine cursed David by his gods. And the Philistine said to David, "Come to me, and I will give your flesh to the birds of the air and the beasts of the field!" Then David said to the Philistine, "You come to me with a sword, with a spear, and with a javelin. But I come to you in the name of the Lord of hosts, the God of the armies of Israel, whom you have defied. This day the Lord will deliver you into my hand, and I will strike you and take your head from you. And this day I will give the carcasses of the camp of the Philistines to the birds of the air and the wild beasts of the earth, that all the earth may know that there is a God in Israel. Then all this assembly shall know that the Lord does not save with sword and spear; for the battle is the Lord's, and He will give you into our hands." (1 Samuel 17:38-47)

Living in our society today has truly become a challenge for so many, mainly about personal identities. Comparing oneself to another human being seems to be the order of the day. It appears to me that people always look for validation, so they constantly look around to see who is like them or compares to them. I believe you know what I'm talking about.

Now, I am not saying that the need to feel a sense of belonging or validation began yesterday; I just haven't seen how much the need for it has increased in the last few years, especially through social media.

Social media has its benefits, and God can use it, but it also has its negative side, especially when it deals with man's character and value. It can affect our personality, our character, and our moral standards.

The interest of people to look their best, to be their best, to dress their best, to pursue their dreams, and to be a better version of themselves is in the interest of many social media forums. People can't stop comparing themselves with others!

A few days ago, I was sitting at a local coffee shop when I noticed this young lady come in and sit next to my table. Suddenly, she pulled out her phone and started taking pictures of herself and posting them on the internet—yes, for all the world to see.

I was so tempted to ask her why she was doing that. What was the point of sending pictures of herself for all to see? How many photos does one have to pose and upload to feel accepted, wanted, appreciated, and loved? Do people have that much power over your life? What happened to the idea of becoming a person of value or character?

Our society is definitely changing at a very rapid pace, and unless we grasp the values we believe we have, we will also be carried away.

David Knew God's Blueprint!

In pondering the changes happening in our society today, I was reminded of little David, who would later become the King of Israel.

You see, David had been a worshipper and a warrior since he was young. The story in 1 Samuel 17:34-36 gives us a brief resume of his life, "But David said to Saul, "Your servant used to keep his father's sheep, and when a lion or a bear came and took a lamb out of the flock, I went out after it and struck it, and delivered the lamb from its mouth; and when it arose against me, I caught it by its beard, and struck and killed it. Your servant has killed both lion and bear, and this uncircumcised Philistine will be like one of them, seeing he has defied the armies of the living God."

David was a man touched by God and knew of God's faithfulness to him. David knew of the favor of God and the power of God. He didn't doubt God's blessing over his life. He knew God had made him, "**I will praise You, for I am fearfully and wonderfully made; Marvelous are Your works, And that my soul knows very well.**" (Psalm 139:14)

If you don't know who you are, you will never know who God is; if you don't know who God is, you will never know who you are! David knew God!

To a certain extent, society propagates that you can invent, make, or design your own blueprint by doing this or that!

If you love God, then you know who made your blueprint. You want to design your life by this blueprint, not somebody's ideology.

Another Man's Armor

"So, Saul clothed David with his armor and put a bronze helmet on his head; he also clothed him with a coat of mail. David fastened his sword to his armor and tried to walk, for he had not tested them. And David said to Saul, "I cannot walk with these, for I have not tested them." So, David took them off."

As David was getting ready to fight the giant Goliath, King Saul offered David his armor for battle. Though it was a splendid gesture, David couldn't fit in them, much less walk in them.

I believe one of David's most significant decisions was to "take them off."

Sometimes, we feel that we must wear someone else's anointing. Just remember: God has anointed you. This anointing connects with the person you are, the one God has designed.

Another Man's Weapon

"Then he took his staff in his hand, and he chose for himself five smooth stones from the brook, and put them in a shepherd's bag, in a pouch which he had, and his sling was in his hand."

As believers, we will face many battles; we must always know that God has provided everything we will ever need to win.

I know that sometimes people have ideas on overcoming certain situations, and there may be a lot of truth in what we are instructed to do. However, deposited within every believer is the anointing, the Holy Spirit, which God has given us to lead us in every step of life.

My point is that we must always be in tune with God and aware of all the tools God has given us to fight. God has so wonderfully equipped all of us as His servants that if we ask the Lord for wisdom, He will give it!

David didn't take Saul's sword, the bronze helmet, or any other coverings; David took what he was acquainted with, and this included his staff, five smooth stones from the brook, a shepherd's bag (pouch,) and a sling.

Be Yourself!

In closing this devotion, a few things come to my mind. One of these is that the exact way God made you and me is how He plans to use us. He has placed gifts, talents, abilities, and excellent qualities that fit us.

Trying to be like someone and attempting to be a copycat version of someone's life or journey would only lead us to frustration. People around us can inspire us, and I'm all for that, but to try to be led by someone else's vision, purpose, or anointing would be short-changing the great things God wants to do in us and through us. Neh'enah.

11

It's Time to Graduate from Kindergarten!

When the Lord tests a soul, he usually does so to produce a change in his servants.

All testing has great significance to God, for through testing, He longs to accomplish some much-needed transformation, making that servant a true worshiper and passionate lover of Christ.

Before God can accomplish this transformation, the Spirit of God must deal with some obstacles in the human heart, such as impatience, taking shortcuts, cheating the system, selfish ambition, and the quest for more money and power.

Mankind has never been more vulnerable than when it finds itself drowning in adversity, such as sickness, economic challenges, or the loss of a loved one(s).

Somehow, trials can wake up a part of the human being and begin looking for help from a higher power during these times.

The Coming of the Spiritual Spoiled Brats!

In our society today, people have become enslaved to the idea that promotes entitlements, and thus, when challenged, we don't make the grade. If a fiery trial is testing us, we usually score very poorly. I am speaking of society in general.

Now, the believer has embraced this idea as well.

When being tested, believers walk around "naming and claiming" or making decrees that they find in the Scriptures when they should be getting a hold of God in the secret place of prayer. This is where you get all your answers—did I say ALL your answers?

We have more believers [mind you, they have been saved for years] still whining and complaining about their trials in life.

Either they have a wrong theology about who Jesus Christ is or lack attention and need the pastor to pray for them. I am not against praying for people, but I am against the idea that a believer whines and complains in the flesh and demands to be spared from his hour of testing.

This kind of Christianity hovers over America today and is quickly spreading around the world.

A Season of Confusion!

I was truly lost and confused during a testing season in my life [1999]. I had opened a church in the Spanish language and felt that God was behind it. Of course, it was just a feeling. My wife began to experience adverse effects from this project, and I felt God was saying something serious regarding this work.

One morning, while in prayer, I heard the Lord tell me to shut it down. He told me that He would show me what I was to do in time.

After hearing His voice, I took a Sabbatical, which lasted for nine months. I took some time to pray, fast, and get counsel for my future.

I visited a friend of mine (who lives in Missouri and who I trust with spiritual matters) and spent a few hours with him. I shared my confusion and chaos with him, hoping he would give me a prophetic word or some much-needed direction, and said, "David. If I gave you direction and wise counsel, I might lead you away from what God wants to do in you. I dare not touch it! Go back home and seek God."

This was not what my flesh wanted to hear, but my spirit rejoiced in God, my Savior, for I knew God was not finished with His plans for me. It is sufficient to say that I learned a great lesson!

I share all that to say that when God is leading our lives, He is literally leading us. He is not joking or playing some prank on us. When the Spirit of God came within us, He came to lead us in the ways of Christ. We must always remember this.

What is a Fiery Trial?

"Beloved, do not think it strange concerning the fiery trial, which is to try you, as though some strange thing happened to you; but rejoice to the extent that you partake of Christ's sufferings, that when His glory is revealed, you may also be glad with exceeding joy." (1 Peter 4:12, 13)

Fiery trials are those trials that come our way to try or test us in our character. Our quick response to our adversity tells us where we are with God.

Please know that these trials usually come upon kindergarten Christians. These trials expose the latent or dormant power in us! These trials reveal that ugly thing in all of us called the flesh.

The fiery trials will provoke us to see ourselves as God sees us. Most believers see these trials and start whining. Is it any wonder that their lives never develop; they may develop other areas, but not depth of character.

Seasonal Testing!

Let me share a bit about seasonal testing. Some fiery trials and trials last a season. Fiery trials are usually very short and then pass, but seasonal testing is much longer.

One thing I have noticed about seasonal testing is that, in your heart, you know that God is working in you and all around you. You understand that the outcome of this will be consequential. You know it! It is not a mystery to your spirit man.

The thing about season testing is that it is not for those who are in kindergarten. If you share your experience of what you are facing or going through with a kindergarten Christian, they will say, "You need to have more faith!" or "You are a "child of God," and you don't have to face this!" or "You have the authority to break out of this!" or worse, they will say, "Just confess your victory!" How can you "confess" your victory when the One you are fighting against is God? I mean, are you going to beat God and live? Dumbest thing I have ever heard!

Seasonal testing lasts a season. Who knows how long it will last? My safe guess is that it will last until you learn the lesson! I have been to this place.

We Must Recognize!

People continually go to church for personal prayer, post their needs to other brothers on their chats, and constantly cry about various things. These Kindergarten Christians must be made aware of what the Lord is doing in their lives. It's time to understand God's will! It's time to sit quietly before Him and listen to the only One who holds your life in His hands.

The truth of the matter is that these Kindergarten Christians are forever attempting not to die to their flesh! They are literally expressing without voicing it, "Pray for me because I don't want to go through a season of transformation; I don't want to die to my flesh!"

It is time to graduate from Kindergarten Christianity! Our nation has never needed the real believer to come out of the woodwork and live out His convictions founded after the heart of God.

Meditate on these:

"Now great multitudes went with Him. And He turned and said to them, "If anyone comes to Me and does not hate his father and mother, wife and children, brothers and sisters, yes, and his own life also, he cannot be My disciple." (Luke 14:25, 26)

"Most assuredly, I say to you, unless a grain of wheat falls into the ground and dies, it remains alone; but if it dies, it produces much grain. He who loves his life will lose it, and he who hates his life in this world will keep it for eternal life. If anyone serves Me, let him follow Me; and where I am, there My servant will be also. If anyone serves Me, him My Father will honor." (John 12:24-26) Neh'enah.

12

What Voice Has Our Attention?

"While He was still speaking, some came from the ruler of the synagogue's house who said, "Your daughter is dead. Why trouble the Teacher any further?" As soon as Jesus heard the word that was spoken, He said to the ruler of the synagogue, "Do not be afraid; only believe." And He permitted no one to follow Him except Peter, James, and John the brother of James. Then He came to the house of the ruler of the synagogue and saw a tumult and those who wept and wailed loudly. When He came in, He said to them, "Why make this commotion and weep? The child is not dead but sleeping." And they ridiculed Him. But when He had put them all outside, He took the father and the mother of the child, and those who were with Him, and entered where the child was lying. Then He took the child by the hand, and said to her, "Talitha, cumi," which is translated, "Little girl, I say to you, arise." Immediately the girl arose and walked, for she was twelve years of age. And they were overcome with great amazement." (Mark 5:35-42)

In sharing this truth, the Spirit of God gave me, and I want to open my devotion with the words that came out of one of the servant's mouths, saying, "**Your daughter is dead. Why trouble the Teacher any further?**"

How many times have we heard this same tone of voice?

I believe that this is one of the most vicious voices inspired by death itself. Of course, the ruler's servant only relayed a message to his boss; I don't think he meant anything other than communicating. Yet, it could have changed the outcome of this story.

Many of our stories have been changed by words born in Satan's womb.

Too many destinies have been obstructed because of a lack of discernment.

Many of the voices you and I hear are just that—information! You hear the adverse reports coming from politicians, news media, family, friends, your medical doctor, Christian brothers and sisters, and, of course, the devil himself. How we process this information will make all the difference in our attempt to overcome it.

Do Not Fear!

In an instant, Jesus raised a standard against those damning words and said to the Ruler, **"Do not be afraid; only believe."**

If there were ever a time for the Spirit of God to arise within us, it would be amid a trying moment.

Jesus spoke against those words the very opposite, **"Do not be afraid; only believe."**

The first thing Jesus spoke against these damning words was fear. Fear in this context means to be frightened, to panic, to have terror with the intent to run away. The only way to overcome fear is by God's perfect love! Knowing that your heavenly Father cares about the things that concern you is pure love. When you believe in His love, you won't fear!

Jesus said, **"...only believe!"** Believe means the following: a) Confidence, Trust; b) Trustworthiness, Reliability; c) Assurance.

This is one reason private, personal prayer is so needed, and even more so as we see the days turning more wicked.

Jesus's words are truth and life! If anyone has heard many negative reports lately, it is time to take Jesus' words to heart and believe His testimony!

Are Words Enough?

Sometimes, we are taught to just believe and then discover that nothing has changed. Has this ever happened to you? I have heard many people prophesy stuff like this but to no avail. Why? Where's the miracle? Let's keep hearing the Word of the Lord...

"And He permitted no one to follow Him except Peter, James, and John the brother of James." I don't know about you, but Jesus had His favorites. These were servants who had been with Jesus from the beginning; they followed Him intently and were now called to take care of spiritual business. God will always call those faithful and use them for extraordinary tasks. These are His *Special Forces*.

As they made their way to the ruler's house, people had already gathered to mourn with the family for their loss. Listen to this: **"Then He came to the house of the ruler of the synagogue, and saw a tumult and those who wept and wailed loudly."**

When Jesus showed up, His heart was full of faith and ready to take care of business. This is an attitude that those who know God have. They are prepared to take care of business for God! Jesus said, **"Why make this commotion and weep? The child is not dead but sleeping."** The devil didn't like these words at all!

The Devil Will Fight Back!

Here's what the devil thought of the words of Jesus: **"...And they ridiculed Him."** It isn't always the idea for the devil to look down on your weak faith and mock it? It's such a classic thing of the devil to do.

Jesus didn't even mess with the devil. Here's what He did: **"But when He had put them all outside, He took the father and the mother of the child, and those who were with Him, and entered where the child was** lying. Then He took the child by the hand, and said to her, "Talitha, cumi," which is translated, "Little girl, I say to you, arise." Immediately, the girl arose and walked, for she was twelve years of age."

My dear friend, here is the recipe for revival in your life. Please eliminate anything that is a negative thought and put it outside of your life. It may cost you some friends, etc., but it must be done if you want to see God move!

Notice how Jesus took the parents and three disciples, all people of faith. The special forces must take their rightful place if you want to accomplish anything. Surround yourself with such men and women of God. Neh'en-ah.

13

Enabled!

"And I thank Christ Jesus our Lord who has enabled me, because He counted me faithful, putting me into the ministry, although I was formerly a blasphemer, a persecutor, and an insolent man; but I obtained mercy because I did it ignorantly in unbelief. And the grace of our Lord was exceedingly abundant, with faith and love which are in Christ Jesus. This is a faithful saying and worthy of all acceptance that Christ Jesus came into the world to save sinners, of whom I am chief. However, for this reason, I obtained mercy, that in me first Jesus Christ might show all longsuffering, as a pattern to those who are going to believe in Him for everlasting life. Now, to the King eternal, immortal, invisible, and to God who alone is wise, be honor and glory forever and ever. Amen. (1 Timothy 1:12-17)

This must be one of the greatest love stories ever told when we think of salvation and how God pulled us out of the miry clay. We all have our own story as we yield our lives to Jesus Christ, who is now our Lord.

Like you and me, the Apostle Paul has a story to tell about his encounter with Christ.

His transformation was profound due to his pride, rebellion, and stubborn will. Does this sound familiar? Our stories are close to his. Thanks be to God for showing us mercy and saving us.

Enabled!

In the Scripture above, the Apostle Paul mentions how God enabled him. Enabled means "one who has an ability, a capacity, or power" and "one who is powerful."

One point to notice is that Saul of Tarsus was a young man brought up in the teachings of the Torah and educated in the Law of Moses by Gamaliel. Saul of Tarsus had a passion for studying God's words. Did God consider this when he called Saul of Tarsus into His service? Perhaps.

I believe God saw this young man and, by His sovereign power, led him all through his life until he was saved.

Sometimes, we look at someone's life and wonder if they have hope and a future. The answer is yes! Jesus has come to destroy the works of the devil and establish His kingdom in people's hearts. This means He has come to demolish the will of the flesh and establish His perfect will in everyone who accepts Him into their hearts.

Our Purpose

As I unfold this truth, I want you to notice how the Lord walks with us throughout our lives. From the day we are born, one must realize that God had a purpose and a design for us before our mother's womb.

The Lord didn't begin His work when we were in our mother's womb; He started this work when He first thought of giving us a purpose. By the time my mother and father met, God already had our design in mind.

It is safe to say that God had something in His heart and needed a vessel to carry these wishes out. Guess what? He chose you and me! We were born because of God's desire, not by mistake.

This is one of the reasons that abortion is such a wicked thing in our society today. The taking of a life, which begins at conception, is murder.

The devil intends to destroy life, the life that God has designed for His will and purposes, and His good pleasure. The taking of a life is plain murder!

Enabled to Live for God!

When we are given life, we initially begin life under the care of our parents. They feed us and take care of us, and we are dependent upon them for our care. In our development stage, we demonstrate characteristics embedded in our DNA.

As we continue to grow and mature, our design takes shape. We develop habits, skills, and attitudes and begin to move according to our understanding of life. Our natural gifts, given by God, begin to develop as well. Up to this point, we are enabled by our natural life.

It is not until we come to Christ in complete surrender that our natural gifts find their true meaning. The minute we realize that we were endowed with natural abilities and that it was God who gave them for His purpose, desire, and good pleasure, that is when our lives truly begin to have meaning. It is a beautiful thing!

Like you and I, Paul was enabled by God from birth.

He was given natural abilities and gifts, just like you and me. He grew and developed His natural skills by living in his culture. You and I, just like Paul, have also been allowed to live a fruitful life.

It's in the Recognition!

When Jesus touched Paul's life in the Book of Acts, he was enabled from the natural into the supernatural - think about that.

You and I also have this access. Once we recognize that God has given us gifts and skills and acknowledge fully that these [gifts] came from Him and for Him, our lives will never be the same! Neh'enah.

14

The Few!

"For many are called, but few are chosen." (Matthew 22:14)

In our meditation today, I want to point out the situation before us. Jesus invited people to a banquet, but they didn't come. Why? People didn't go to it because they were preoccupied with other priorities, and following Jesus was not one of them! It's that simple.

This same example continues to be lived out by many today as they continue to show self over the will of God.

Many preachers and teachers have avoided the subject of commitment to Christ for salvation, service, and ministry in an effort not to offend anyone.

For those who accept Christ's will for their lives, there is no need to feel like they are the only ones serving Christ with full-hearted devotion. You must know that God has always had these two veins of thought proposed by His creation as humanity makes a choice whether to serve Him with full-hearted devotion or not.

When I think of servants who served God in their generation, I think of people like Noah, Abraham, Moses, and David. All these servants had a choice to serve themselves but chose God instead.

Think of it:

God told Noah to build an ark: **"And God said to Noah, "The end of all flesh has come before Me, for the earth is filled with violence through** them; and behold, I will destroy them with the earth. Make yourself an ark..." (Genesis 6:13, 14).

In the book of Hebrews, we see a deeper meaning to this encounter: "By faith Noah, being divinely warned of things not yet seen, moved with godly fear, prepared an ark for the saving of his household, by which he condemned the world and became heir of the righteousness which is according to faith." (Hebrews 11:7)

We see Abraham following the voice of God in Genesis 12:1-4. It was God's heart to make a nation by using Abraham. God would have chosen someone else if Abraham hadn't obeyed the Lord.

In matters of choice, we also see the life of Moses as an example. Moses was living the good life in the palace of the king. He did not need to do anything for anyone but himself. Yet, when Moses came of age, something transpired within him. Listen to this: "By faith Moses, when he became of age, refused to be called the son of Pharaoh's daughter, choosing rather to suffer affliction with the people of God than to enjoy the passing pleasures of sin, esteeming the reproach of Christ greater riches than the treasures in Egypt; for he looked to the reward. By faith, he forsook Egypt, not fearing the wrath of the king; for he endured as seeing Him who is invisible." (Hebrews 11:24-27)

Chosen for His Task

In the book of Genesis, we find that God had worked for five days and had built an amazing garden, but no one was present to tend to it. It was at this time that God created man. He made man in a certain way. The man was designed by God and for God. The man was not made for himself. He was commissioned to tend to the Garden of Eden.

One thing to notice is that this garden was made for a specific type of man. Man was called out from the dust and created to be a vessel for

God's purpose.

As we followed the story, we learned that the serpent tempted and seduced Adam and Eve. After sinning against God, man lost His essence. Their rebellion against God brought sin into man's heart and was enough to disqualify him from His original purpose. The Lord had no choice but to take man out of the Garden of Eden and put His purpose on hold until His due time.

God's Chosen Vessel

We can look at many qualities in the men and women that God chose and determine that this list of qualities is what God is looking for. Let me just say that these men and women were not finished products when they started. These vessels were fearful, sinful, and filled with every selfish desire known to man, yet they had burning hearts to please God.

Qualities such as godly character, obedience, disposition, sacrifice, and a willingness to give their lives to God were always before them; however, all these came as they stepped out in faith to enter into their promise.

Entering Into His Will

It was God's desire to bring His people out of Egypt and into the land of Canaan, the Promised Land. Through the leadership of Moses and Joshua, God would accomplish this purpose.

Everything appeared to be in place for this to occur when the Hebrew children of Israel met one of their biggest challenges. The challenge was to cross into the Promised Land, but they were overcome with doubt and fear, not to mention rebellion. This got the Lord very angry. [Numbers 13 & 14].

Remember: Some character development lessons will come before we enter His purpose, some will take place during the process, and other tests will come after we live under the blessing of His will.

What Disqualifies Us?

"Therefore, as the Holy Spirit says:
"Today, if you will hear His voice,
Do not harden your hearts as in the rebellion,
In the day of trial in the wilderness,
Where your fathers tested Me, tried Me,
And saw My works forty years.
Therefore I was angry with that generation,
And said, 'They always go astray in their heart,
And they have not known My ways.'
So I swore in My wrath,
'They shall not enter My rest.'"

Beware, brethren, lest there be in any of you an evil heart of unbelief in departing from the living God; but exhort one another daily, while it is called "Today," lest any of you be hardened through the deceitfulness of sin. For we have become partakers of Christ if we hold the beginning of our confidence steadfast to the end, while it is said:

"Today, if you will hear His voice,
Do not harden your hearts as in the rebellion."

For who, having heard, rebelled? Indeed, was it not all who came out of Egypt, led by Moses? Now with whom was He angry forty years? Was it not with those who sinned, whose corpses fell in the wilderness? And to whom did He swear that they would not enter His rest, but to those who did not obey? So, we see that they could not enter in because of unbelief." (Hebrews 3:7-19)

What is the disqualifying factor? By reading the Scripture, nothing disqualifies us from entering God's rest, God's will, or God's perfect plan for us like this one verse:

"Therefore, I was angry with that generation,
And said, 'They always go astray in their heart,
And they have not known My ways.'
So, I swore in My wrath,
'They shall not enter My rest.'"

What does it mean to **"always go astray in our hearts?"** It means that we have not decided to learn the ways of God, and we continually keep going back to our fleshly lifestyle; we continually keep falling away into our stubborn ways and not walking according to God's divine ways.

As this meditation ends, take the time to search and evaluate your heart before the presence of Jesus. Is there something disqualifying you from entering God's rest or God's best? Neh'enah.

15

Going Outside the Camp!

"Then Moses said to the Lord, "See, You say to me, 'Bring up this people.' But You have not let me know whom You will send with me. Yet You have said, 'I know you by name, and you have also found grace in My sight.' Now therefore, I pray, if I have found grace in Your sight, show me now Your way, that I may know You and that I may find grace in Your sight. And consider that this nation is Your people."
And He said, "My Presence will go with you, and I will give you rest."
Then he said to Him, "If Your Presence does not go with us, do not bring us up from here. For how then will it be known that Your people and I have found grace in Your sight, except You go with us? So we shall be separate [distinct], Your people and I, from all the people who are upon the face of the earth." (Exodus 33:12-16)

Moses, the man of God, reached a point in His leadership when God's people were just plain rebellious and headed nowhere fast without God. The children of Israel had just been rebuked for making a golden calf, and God wasn't having it!

The Lord had made up His mind about judging the Hebrew children, and Moses attempted to change God's mind. Despite this, God didn't change His plans for His people. He told them to keep marching forward.

"Then the Lord said to Moses, "Depart and go up from here, you and the people whom you have brought out of the land of Egypt, to the land of which I swore to Abraham, Isaac, and Jacob, saying, 'To your descendants, I will give it.' And I will send My Angel before you, and I will drive out the Canaanite and the Amorite and the Hittite and the Perizzite and the Hivite and the Jebusite. Go up to a land flowing with milk and honey." (Exodus 3:1-3)

The command to follow God's leadership was before them. The fact that some didn't follow God's orders and turned to idol worship didn't change God's plan for the faithful few. God still had a mission to accomplish.

The Tent of Meeting

"Moses took his tent and pitched it outside the camp, far from the camp, and called it the tabernacle of meeting. And it came to pass that everyone who sought the Lord went out to the tabernacle of meeting which was outside the camp." (Exodus 33:7)

The Tent of Meeting was where Moses met God face to face. It is a type of altar, the prayer closet, if you will. Everyone must have a prayer closet to meet God and hear His heart.

It doesn't matter what happens in or around us; we must enter our Tent of Meeting. We must meet with God face to face. Without His presence, we will not make it!

In Prayer, You Will See Your Inward Parts!

I recently met God in prayer and poured out my heart before Him, Allowing Him to bathe me with His presence and search my inward parts. The more I prayed, the more I realized how cold and indifferent I had become in my walk and service to Him.

Now, don't get me wrong. I still pray and preach and teach. I witness every time I get a chance and counsel the ones in need. The outward portion is still there, but not the inward. The anointing, the brokenness, and the passion to become more and more like Jesus were running low, and the Lord allowed me to see it.

I believe Moses got to a spiritual place in God where he must have said, "I need God!" I need to get back to His presence. I need His presence!"

Just listen to His humble cry: "Then Moses said to the Lord, "See, You say to me, 'Bring up this people.' But You have not let me know whom You will send with me. Yet You have said, 'I know you by name, and you have also found grace in My sight.' Now therefore, I pray, if I have found grace in Your sight, show me now Your way, that I may know You and that I may find grace in Your sight. And consider that this nation is Your people." And He said, "My Presence will go with you, and I will give you rest." Then he said to Him, "If Your Presence does not go with us, do not bring us up from here. For how then will it be known that Your people and I have found grace in Your sight, except You go with us? So we shall be separate [distinct], Your people and I, from all the people who are upon the face of the earth." (Exodus 33:12-16)

The Need for His Presence.

God's presence is a must for every servant of God. You can't minister in God's power without it. You don't become distinct without His presence. Throughout my service unto the Lord, I have discovered that the first thing a man loses when God's presence is gone is his discernment. You slowly begin to move in the flesh without even recognizing it.

Now, leaving the camp is not easy. It's important, and probably the place where you must find yourself to meet God, but as valuable as it is, the flesh doesn't like it. This is why many church leaders don't pray.

As much as I appreciate psychology and am thankful for the people who practice it, most issues are not mental but spiritual. The root cause is usually hidden behind our disobedience caused by our unruly flesh, which people don't want to crucify [see Galatians 2:20].

Now, if we can enter the Tent of Meeting and prostrate ourselves before

God, we will have an encounter.

Here are a few things we will receive if we walk in His presence:

1. Direction; vision; the ability to see where one needs to go through. God's presence is not a feeling, a sensation, or even a cloud upon your head; His presence is His very nature in you. You are carrying the life of Another within you - His life!

2. We will move in God's favor as we walk in His presence. Knowing that you are doing what He told you to do guarantees favor. His favor strengthens our spirit and affects our emotions.

3. Provision is also received when His presence accompanies you. Confidence, peace, boldness, and authority will be your portion. With provision, you will lack any good thing.

To those who seek the face of God and allow God to do His mighty work in them, blessing will follow them. True joy will be their portion. Neh'en-ah.

16

Time to Watch!

"Take heed, watch and pray; for you do not know when the time is. It is like a man going to a far country, who left his house and gave authority to his servants, and to each his work, and commanded the doorkeeper to watch. Watch therefore, for you do not know when the master of the house is coming—in the evening, at midnight, at the crowing of the rooster, or in the morning—lest, coming suddenly, he find you sleeping. And what I say to you, I say to all: Watch!" (Mark 13:32-37)

The Walk of Faith

Walking with God when you don't feel or see something can be challenging. People are always looking for signs to keep themselves encouraged. Others seek prophetic words to keep them in the flow of faith. In many cases, others are temporarily urged by all the church's activities.

My dear friends, let me remind you of what Paul said regarding our walk.

In 2 Corinthians, Paul says, "**For we walk by faith, not by sight** [living our lives in a manner consistent with our confident belief in God's promises]." (2 Corinthians 5:7 AMP). In walking with God, one must understand that it is only through the Spirit of the Lord that lives within that affirms us and confirms that we are His children.

The abiding in Christ and He abiding in us is the key to a successful Christian walk in God. Without this happening in us, we are doomed from the beginning.

We come to Christ because we have accepted that we are sinners, undone and without God in the world. Only through Christ can we regain our position, which God initially gave us from the foundations of the world.

If one trusts their emotions, one will set themselves up for failure. The consequence of all this outward motivation will, sooner than later, fade away. You see, the servant who is not walking by faith, who the Spirit does not lead, will find himself falling away from the church programs and the church altogether.

If the Spirit of God is not keeping you strong and empowered in God, you will be in trouble. You cannot follow God in the flesh – not only is it hard, but it is also impossible!

Jesus Commands Us to Watch!

When Jesus shares His heart in this parable regarding this man who went off to a far country and left his house under the care and authority of his servants, and further commanded them to watch, for they needed to be watching when he would return, he didn't tell them the time of his return.

The inference was that the servants would not be found sleeping. The warning for believers is the same: Watch, lest he come suddenly and find us sleeping!

Things that Put Us to Sleep!

Some things lull us to sleep; even the strongest believers can fall into this slumber. Let me share some things that may come upon a godly servant and put him to sleep.

The first thing on this list is pride. The sin of pride is a big one. Many people think they are super spiritual, and such slumber couldn't reach them. But let me tell you, nothing is more deceiving than spiritual pride. For one, the Apostle Paul warned those in Corinth regarding pride. Here is what Paul admonished: "**Therefore let the one who thinks he stands firm** [immune to temptation, being overconfident and self-righteous], **take care that he does not fall** [into sin and condemnation]." (1 Corinthians 10:12 AMP)

Thinking one is immune to failure or temptation, and even assuming he is self-righteous, is a perfect recipe for disgrace. Many have fallen into this pit.

The second thing on this list is overconfidence. Many servants of God never think that their sins will find them out. It doesn't take much for God to bring this man to a place where his overconfidence will be his stumbling block. Once a person begins to feel overconfident, the enemy has gotten you! It is only a matter of time before you will experience a fall.

Finally, the third thing that puts you to sleep is a lack of personal prayer. I believe that when a man stops praying, he starts to sin. The same is true when a man begins praying; he will stop sinning.

When prayer is absent, this is man's way of saying, "I don't need God's help. I can do it all by myself." No sooner does a man think more highly of himself when suddenly he will find himself under a spirit of slumber overwhelming his life and ministry.

Only through prayer can we stay engaged with God and stay informed about what He is doing in the world.

Let us stay awake; the greatest hour is yet to be! Neh'enah.

17

It's Time to Examine Ourselves!

"Examine yourselves to see whether you are in the faith. Test yourselves. Or do you not realize this about yourselves, that Jesus Christ is in you? —unless indeed you fail to meet the test!" (2 Corinthians 13:5 ESV)

In reaching this truth today, I want to highlight the importance of personal evaluation. Why is it valuable, and how often should one assess himself individually?

Definition of the Word *examine.*

Before I proceed with my subject, let us examine 2 Corinthians 13:5 and study the word examine.

It means "to attempt," "to strive," "to make an effort," b. "to put to the test." Also, "to try someone," "to put to the test," almost always in an expression of distrust." Also, "To test a thing" in order to assess its value.

One thing I have noticed when I have spoken to individuals is that most people don't dare to examine their own lives. Many are too busy examining other people's lives to realize how pointless it is to compare oneself to others.

Now, examining oneself is a challenging feat. Many people don't do it for fear of what they may discover. Others don't do it due to simple pride. The idea is that they are complete in themselves and don't need to look any further for imperfections. I am sure you have met characters such as these.

All change starts in the heart of man. Many may think that change occurs by fate; they believe things shift or change like nature. For example, the leaves that turn color on trees, etc. Nature has its way of changing, but so do human beings.

Our Society

When the Word of God is the standard by which one lives his or her life, the outcome of a prosperous and blessed life will be the outcome. Those who put their faith in a risen Savior and have complete confidence in His Words will also reap the benefits of their faith.

If your ideals are not biblical but only ideas birthed in the heart of fallen man, the results will be corrupt and eventually pass away.

Many of the influential people in America are not people of faith. They have faith, but not in Jesus Christ or His Word. Their faith is mostly in themselves. Therefore, their thinking is perverted and not God-pleasing.

Due to this rampant rebellion towards God and His holy Word, society has been impacted by "the rebellion." These are those who walk in the flesh and practice lawlessness – it is those who believe in homosexuality as an alternate lifestyle and applaud sin. These are the same ones that Isaiah called out, saying, **"Woe unto them that call evil good, and good evil; that put darkness for light, and light for darkness; that put bitter for sweet, and sweet for bitter!"** (Isaiah 5:20)

During our latest presidential election, I heard many people speak about not needing to change anything in our society. They felt that what they were holding on to was perfect the way it was. What was even sadder to me was how many so-called Bible believers who adhere to the Biblical teachings of Christ fell into the trap of following such wicked thinking in our society.

It's Personal!

Moving from our society's viewpoint, let us look at our personal lives and examine them.

I'm of the idea that if society is terrible, the church is terrible! If the church is lacking, our society will be lacking, too.

You see, our spiritual walk dictates our lives; our lives impact society, and society will affect our generations.

How is your spiritual life? If we let go of our responsibility to follow hard after God, we will efficiently and quickly fall out of God's design. Is it any wonder why people live such cold and indifferent lives towards God and humanity? Our streets have become a living hell. There is much rampant disorder, and it all points to lawlessness.

Without a true passion for the Lord, what else do we have? Our desires will be worldly, our ambitions will be selfish, and our pursuit will be selfish gain only.

Time For God to Search Us!

Let us humble ourselves in the sight of the Lord and ask Him to search us. This was David's prayer; listen to it: **"Search me, O God, and know my heart: try me, and know my thoughts: And see if there be any wicked way in me and lead me in the way everlasting."** (Psalm 139:23, 24)

How am I doing with my stand on holiness toward God? Am I seeking to please Him with my whole being? Do I still believe that I was created by Him and for Him? Am I walking in the calling God has destined for me, or am I doing my own thing? Am I being an ambassador for Him and a light to people and the nations? Do I thank God for all I have and give my tithes to Him? When I vote for city, state, and national officials, do I vote with Christian principles in view?

These are some things to consider as we go forward in His Name. Neh'en-ah.

18

The One and Only Key to Overcoming Fear!

"There we saw the giants (the descendants of Anak came from the giants), and we were like grasshoppers in our own sight, and so we were in their sight." (Numbers 13:33)

It is a true statement when one says that fear is an emotion that has kept many under wraps. Fear has kept people from moving forward and many from advancing into more excellent opportunities.

In my short time of knowing God's heart, I have discovered that fear is accurate and that all that has been taught about it is true. It keeps people from moving forward.

I know this to be true, for I have succumbed to the voice of fear, and I cannot even begin to tell you of the countless opportunities fear has taken away from me.

In retrospect, I must ask myself, in the most honest of ways, who is to blame for my lack of advancement: Is it fear? Or is it me?

Psychology of Fear

Let me share a few thoughts on this.

The *Oxford Dictionary* defines fear as *an unpleasant emotion caused by the belief that someone or something is dangerous, likely to cause pain or a threat.*

Fear is an emotion in the mind that sends a message to you and me of oncoming danger. So, to avoid the threat or the risk, we don't follow the thing that produces this emotion, not caring whether the thing, as a result, is good or bad. Do you get me? We would instead discard the whole idea behind the emotion of fear! This, we would conclude, is a better path for us.

Whatever your decision might be, it will produce a result; you will have to live with the decision that gave that result.

In the natural [differentiating from the spiritual], fear is damming for both the physical and the spiritual dimensions.

Countless life-development gurus and coaches have researched the subject of fear. Many have discovered answers to overcoming fear; however, fear continues to live on, and many still fall prey to it.

Overcoming Fear is More than An Achievement!

Let me try to explain my viewpoint on fear.

In the natural [not spiritual], many believe that fear is a thing to overcome by simply coming up with a recipe that beats it. I get this. But that fear is natural. You see, fear comes to us only when our lives feel threatened. It doesn't show up in any other way. Fear grips us when it comes to costing us more than we can afford.

Let me explain it this way:

When someone says, "I want to cross that river by swimming across, but I am afraid of the undertow or current to carry me away." What this individual is saying without saying it is the following: "I am afraid to be taken by the river's current and drowning and dying!" Do you see this?

It is our life that we are trying to save; fear is not about anything else.

Let us look at the person who says, "I want to cross that river, and I am going for it. I am afraid, but I will do it anyway!" The man jumps into the river, and after struggling time and time again, he finally makes it to the other side. As he gets out of the water, people pat him on the back for such a feat. The people are impressed, and the swimmer is full of himself; some call it pride.

Crossing a river and defeating the odds is not eliminating your fear; it will only make you proud and arrogant! You didn't succumb to fear, but you were overcome by pride and arrogance. Which of these things please God?

Many think that fear can be overcome by climbing a mountain, swimming across a river, jumping off a plane, or opening a business; granted, all these have their way of producing fear in us, but this is not the fear the Bible talks about.

Spiritual Fear

Spiritual fear will only appear when God tells you to step into the unknown part of His will. Yes, God will call you to take steps into the impossible, and no one can help you with this. You must know that the only sign you will receive is the faith of God downloaded into your spirit man, your inner man.

For His will to be worked out in our lives, we must be aligned and in tune with God's Holy Spirit. God desires our life to advance according to His design. Due to this, He will bring us into situations that will require us to deal with fear.

Spiritual Fear Exposed!

Spiritual fear is exposed whenever God asks us to walk into the unknown. We are used to walking by sight and get so used to this that when the Holy

Spirit invites us to "cross a river," we begin to fear. Here's where this hidden and latent fear has been hiding - in our flesh.

Let us look at a Biblical story in the Book of Numbers 13:33.

God had ordered the children of Israel to cross the River Jordan into the Promised Land and take their rightful possession. This didn't seem hard at first, but as they got closer to the banks of the river, God was gracious enough and had them send spies to go and check out the land before crossing the river.

After forty days, the spies came back with a mixed report. The land was good as promised, but there were also tribes and giants. This wasn't what they expected, but God knew what was in their hearts and used this experience to expose it, allowing them to see their feeble condition.

One of them said, **"There we saw the giants (the descendants of Anak came from the giants), and we were like grasshoppers in our own sight, and so we were in their sight."**

When they saw the enemy up close, it changed everything!

They first saw them [the giants], then they saw themselves. Their conclusion based on natural sight alone was that we looked like grasshoppers in their sight, and so we were!

At this time, fear gripped their hearts! This is the fear that we are talking about. The fear that comes through the natural eye awakens the fear in the "old man" and paralyzes the faith of God, or at least challenges it. Here's where you and I have found ourselves many times.

Overcoming Fear God's Way

Overcoming fears of heights can be done by climbing a mountain or getting on a plane; overcoming the fear of snakes can be overcome by handling one, or overcoming the fear of swimming can be done by jumping in the water after swimming lessons.

Now, overcoming the fear that comes from within can only be overcome by dying to self. Self must die! The fear that grips us as we try to follow God's will involves saving our lives. So long as we try to play it safe with our lives, we cannot enter His perfect design for us!

Listen to this: **"Then Jesus said to His disciples, "If anyone desires to come after Me, let him deny himself, and take up his cross, and follow Me. For whoever desires to save his life will lose it, but whoever loses his life for My sake will find it. For what profit is it to a man if he gains the whole world and loses his own soul? Or what will a man give in exchange for his soul?"** (Matthew 16:24-27)

We discover that one can only be a disciple of Christ if one is willing to carry His cross and die to self. He cannot be trusted with God's riches. He will be a follower in name only but no further.

The only ones who can follow the Lord are the ones who have died to self, for it is the only way to overcome fear!

Remember, fear is spiritual, embedded in our old man, and will appear anytime God wants us to advance His cause on earth. You can't cast it out; you can only die to it!

When we finally get to this place in God and die to our flesh [Galatians 2:20], then and only then will we start living for Jesus!

We must come to an end of ourselves if we are to enter His life! Nehemiah.

19

Creator of a Clean Heart! Part 1

"Create in me a clean heart, O God,
And renew a steadfast spirit within me." (Psalm 51:10)

Psalm 51 is the one Psalm where King David is confronted by the Prophet Nathan after committing his sin of adultery. As if that sin wasn't enough to hide his adultery, he orders Bathsheba's husband to be killed in battle as well. First adultery and then murder. Can you fathom this?

I know that David wasn't happy about his sins and tried for a while to keep them hidden; this is all too typical of any person who sins against a holy God. I venture to say that there is no feeling that compares to this.

As David lived out his days, the conviction of the Holy Spirit began to be felt more and more. Have you ever been to this place?

Listen to David's song:

When I kept silent, my bones grew old
Through my groaning all the day long.
For day and night Your hand was heavy upon me;
My vitality was turned into the drought of summer.
Selah

I acknowledged my sin to You,
And my iniquity I have not hidden.
I said, "I will confess my transgressions to the Lord,"
And You forgave the iniquity of my sin." (Psalm 32:3-5)

When a servant finally confesses to the Lord any sin that the Holy Spirit has highlighted, the incredible feeling of freedom that true repentance brings must be one of the most remarkable experiences in the human heart.

David said in Psalm 32 that his bones grew old as he groaned all day long. So, imagine the guilt and the shame! He felt the hand of the Lord heavy upon him and felt defeated as his vitality had turned into the summer drought. May God have mercy on us.

Then, after fighting with his conscience and coming to terms with God's conviction, he acknowledged his sin and didn't keep anything hidden from the Lord. This was the beginning of a great revival in David's life.

Forgiving Oneself!

After sins have been committed against God and other people, there is a tremendous feeling of shame, disgust, failure, and dread. You tell yourself repeatedly why you did what you did. As the days turn weeks and weeks into months, you know something is not right in your heart.

Externally, everything may still be in place, but inwardly, something has transpired. Things are not the same anymore. You know you have offended God and must make amends. You understand that the only thing that removes this awful sinking feeling is repentance and getting washed in the blood of Jesus. So you make your way to the altar of the Lord and, with bitter weeping, make your prayers of confession.

As soon as the prayers of repentance come from your heart to the very throne of God, your sins are forgiven. As far as the east is from the west, your sins are separated from you. You have been justified immediately by the power of the blood of Jesus. Hallelujah.

Though you have been forgiven, a small voice comes to you denouncing you by saying, "You are guilty, and you should be ashamed of yourself – you loser! Don't think that coming to Christ to be washed by His blood is enough for your wickedness. He has not forgiven you! Your sin is way bigger, darker, and damaging than any other sin. You are done!"

My dear friends, please understand that from the moment you asked God to forgive you for your sin(s) – the work was immediately heard and done! His blood cleansed you.

Now, forgiving yourself for the wrong committed is where the real dogfight will be. The enemy of your soul will not let it go. He [the devil, the accuser of the Bretheren] will continually upload your failures to your mind and cause you to doubt what Christ has done for you.

Here's where you realize that it is not in your strength, your faith, or your own doing that justifies you, but in Christ alone. Listen to what the beloved disciple John said, **"If we confess our sins, He is faithful and just to forgive us our sins and to cleanse us from all unrighteousness."** (1 John 1:9)

If you have confessed your sins [this is your part], if you have done this, then God does His part: to forgive you and cleanse you of all unrighteousness. In the latter part of this verse, you must believe. You must enter it by faith! No amount of convincing or talking yourself into believing will do; the Holy Spirit must register this in your heart for it to work.

As we enter the subject of how God restores and creates in us a clean heart, keep in mind that restoration is a process that begins with the first baby step of repentance. Once we repent and deal with the voices of guilt and shame brought to us by not forgiving ourselves, we will be on our way to complete restoration. Neh'enah.

20

Creator of a Clean Heart! Part 2

**"Create in me a clean heart, O God,
And renew a steadfast spirit within me."** (Psalm 51:10)

As I continue with this excellent thought in what true repentance brings and how God is determined to restore our weary souls, allow me to open the Scriptures again and share my heart on the subject...

As I mentioned, true repentance opens the highway to God's mind and heart. Our hearts, minds, bodies, and surroundings become tumultuous without genuine repentance. Is it any wonder why some feel sick and isolated? Is there a reason why some people stay away from God's house?

Adam and Eve stayed away from the Lord in Genesis 3 – all because of sin and compromise. When we sin, we hide. This is the enemy's desire for everyone who sins against a loving Father.

An interesting thing about repentance is what happens after we do it. You will know how genuine our repentance has been by the wicked voice of the enemy coming to taunt us and making us doubt what we have just confessed. Yes, to make us feel unworthy.

You see, once we repent, we will deal with the enemy's voice; he will always do everything he can to keep us bound to failure(s). We must enter Christ and His finished work on the cross.

Creating a New Heart

When David prayed to God and pleaded with Him, saying, **"Create in me a clean heart..." what was David saying? He was pleading from a heart of anguish to restore what he felt had been lost. Have you ever experienced such pain? This is true repentance.

David, in essence, was saying to the Lord, *"Lord, I hate what I have done; my heart deceived me, and I need you to create or recreate a new heart that is not full of pride and selfishness!"* Have you ever prayed such a prayer? You can't wait to erase the failure and get a new start.

When a servant understands that His heart is the center of God's presence and realizes that he has messed up this holy place, great remorse will overtake him. This is normal to a heart that walks close to the heart of Jesus.

I don't believe David set himself to fail God; I don't believe this for one minute. However, David's fleshly desires took over, and David found himself in a valley of decision. He chose the way of a transgressor and was now a victim of condemnation, guilt, and shame! This is not a very good place to be.

Can you see why David is now pleading with God and asking God to create a new heart in him?

Renew a Right Spirit!

After pleading for a new heart, David added, **"Renew a right or steadfast spirit within me."** David told God, *"Give me a heart that will never fail you again - I don't want to displease you again, oh God!"*

It wasn't enough to ask God to create a new heart; David also needed a steadfast spirit to continue the path of righteousness. We must pray in that manner as well.

Interestingly, once we align ourselves with God by being justified by the blood of the Lamb, the relationship between us and the Holy Spirit is restored. He is not mad at you; He is not pushing us away because we failed God; the Spirit of God draws near and continues to uphold us as we continue our journey to becoming more like Christ.

People around you may not feel the same about you as God does but know that God has established you under His wings and will keep you till the end. Walking with God is truly a personal walk.

To renew our communion with the Holy Spirit must also be addressed. We must repent before God, forgive ourselves, and then turn to the Spirit of God and lean on His wisdom and guidance in every area of our lives.

It doesn't have to be an emotional experience; enough is to know that He has heard your cry and has seen your repentance. God will take care of the rest if we trust Him!

If you have suffered a failure or are trying to overcome a particular sin(s) today, pray with me: *"King Jesus, I come to you as I am. I want to confess my failure, my compromise, my sin. I know I have displeased you and gone astray in my heart and spirit. Wash my guilty stains with your precious blood so I may stand before you, justified, pure, and holy once again. Will you create a new heart and spirit within me, a heart set upon you every second of my life? Thank you, Jesus, for restoring my heart today. I receive your forgiveness now."* Amen.

21

Creator of a Clean Heart! Part 3

"Do not cast me away from Your presence,
And do not take Your Holy Spirit from me.
Restore to me the joy of Your salvation,
And uphold me by Your generous Spirit." (Psalm 51:11, 12)

Here are some things to learn from true repentance.

As we have begun our journey after repentance, we will continue this restoration process by continual brokenness before God. At times, our journey with God will seem complicated; other times, it will seem like we can genuinely flow in this with no problem.

Once David had opened his heart fully to God and had poured his soul before Him, David began to make amends. He started asking God to restore his heart, spirit, etc.

A thing to know when you come before the Lord in true repentance from the heart is that your spirit will tell you exactly all that you need to ask for. He will show you where you went wrong, what you are missing, and how to get it back. Coming before the Lord with a pure heart begins a life transformation.

It would be wise always to remember how vital it is for a man of God to come clean before the Lord and to plea with God for complete restoration of all that has been lost, mainly his connection method.

His Presence!

Understanding David's request regarding God's presence is of utmost importance. David was a man after God's heart and depended upon God's presence to keep living.

To be in God's presence was David's one desire; He never wanted to be separated from God's awesome presence. He knew that sin had somehow damaged that connection and didn't want to spend another day thinking of what it would mean to be without it.

I have noticed that in many believers, the presence of God is not a big deal. For one, they have never experienced a visitation from the Lord. They don't know Him. So, to be without it is not a big deal, being that they have never experienced such ecstasy.

That is why many so-called user-friendly churches are just social clubs. People go to gatherings for religious purposes, not for encounters of the Godkind. The only reason pastors have church programs and put out their best creative efforts is to make people comfortable and keep them entertained; it is all due to the lack of the presence of Jesus in their meetings. No presence means no power, which, in turn, means no God-given purpose!

David was convinced that if God's presence was not part of His life, there was no reason to continue. Have you ever felt this deep within your own soul?

No Holy Spirit!

"Don't take your Holy Spirit from me."

Would God remove His Spirit from David? We don't know this for sure, but David undoubtedly felt like Something left him after his sinful acts. I think this because otherwise, why would he bring it up in his prayer?

In my personal experience, I know what it is to feel the loss of His Spirit due to my rebellious ways. I know what it means to go without the glory and the Spirit's power for weeks, even months. If you are used to the presence and Spirit of God governing your life and one day you don't feel Him – you will know it!

Restore the Joy!

If there is one thing that true repentance brings, it is joy. The joy of God will flood our hearts once we clear ourselves with God. It is truly a joy unspeakable and full of glory. Nothing can give us this joy like a heart washed by His blood and declared justified by God.

Only when all things are cleared up in heaven will joy be experienced on earth! Joy will always come when our hearts know that God has heard us.

Finally, David prayed, **"And uphold me by Your generous Spirit."** What does this mean? The word uphold in Hebrew means to lean, lay, rest, and support.

In his prayer, David pleaded with the Lord to bring him close to the Spirit so that he could lean, lay, or rest on Him.

When you hear this prayer of true repentance, it is remarkable how detailed David expounds his heart before God and for all generations after him. This is the way to come before the Lord in true repentance if one genuinely desires to restore his life before God.

In closing these devotions on the *Creator of a Clean Heart*, think about your life and where you have been with God.

Are there areas in your life that must be brought up before the Lord and confessed? How about losing His presence in your life, in your walk with Jesus? Do you still have joy in your heart for God? Do you still move by

His Spirit? Do you hear Him leading you? Are you attending church consciously and expecting to meet God face-to-face when you enter the temple? Or is it just plain dead religion all you want?

It is time to consider our ways. Neh'enah.

22

Two Reports!

Who has believed our report? And to whom has the arm of the LORD been revealed?" (Isaiah 53:1)

In our walk with Jesus, if one has genuinely entered His heart and mind, you will discover a whole new way of thinking and living. Before Christ came inside our hearts, we were trapped by our thinking and limited to a life without the power and wisdom of Christ.

The Apostle Paul said, "And you, who once were alienated and enemies in your mind by wicked works, yet now He has reconciled in the body of His flesh through death, to present you holy, and blameless, and above reproach in His sight— if indeed you continue in the faith, grounded and steadfast, and are not moved away from the hope of the gospel which you heard, which was preached to every creature under heaven, of which I, Paul, became a minister." (Colossians 1:21-23)

To follow Jesus is truly an amazing thing, for in it, one will discover a greater fullness of living as His purpose is disclosed through His Word. Where at one point you had nowhere to go, you move with purpose and assurance. This is the beauty of knowing Jesus, the knowledge of God!

The Flesh!

The believer must remember that "the flesh," the carnal man, still resides within but is now under the government of the Spirit of God. Your flesh doesn't govern your life as it used to. You now have the authority to walk in God's footsteps.

Christ in you gives you power and authority to choose God's will for your life.

As you know, the Spirit of God resides within, must be attended to, almost like a barbecue pit, and must be tended with logs and fire fanning. To become negligent with this practice is to commit spiritual suicide.

Prayerless always leads to a life of sin and compromise. Show me someone who doesn't have a personal prayer life, and I'll show you someone who is in bondage to some sin!

Feeding Your Spirit

Feeding your spirit-man, is the key to victory over any situation you might have here on earth. God will unveil things to your heart that He wants you to follow. His Word is Truth, and everything written in it is suitable for instruction.

In following Jesus, we don't follow by mere emotion or guesswork; when we follow Jesus, we know that He is and that He is a Rewarder to those who diligently seek Him.

As you feed your spirit, you will discover peace at such a high level that you won't fear or doubt anything that might come against you.

The Enemy Within

The fact that you know Jesus and that He lives within you doesn't guarantee that the flesh will not try to come from within and present itself as a voice of reason. We tend to reason when external forces are challenging us, thus making us doubt and sometimes wonder if God is in on it.

While believers have been taught to view the devil as the enemy, he is not the one working within your heart; it is your flesh! The flesh begins to challenge our thinking, faith, and doctrine and makes us question our journey.

The Solution!

"I say then: Walk in the Spirit, and you shall not fulfill the lust of the flesh. For the flesh lusts against the Spirit, and the Spirit against the flesh; and these are contrary to one another, so that you do not do the things that you wish." (Galatians 5:16, 17)

Paul teaches much about the spirit and the flesh.

In many of his letters, the Apostle Paul addresses the battle between these two entities that live within us. He boldly speaks of how they are at war and are direct opposites.

In another place, he speaks of the spiritual warfare we fight against, mainly thoughts and arguments birthed in man's mind. These thoughts exalt themselves against the knowledge of Christ and present an antichrist option.

The war against the flesh is a real war that believers must be attentive to. The believer must know that unless he dies to his flesh and carries his cross daily, he will always stumble with fleshly thoughts.

Unless there is an intentional seeking after God and being filled with the Spirit of God continually, it will not be easy to discern the will of the flesh. When our hearts are cold and indifferent, we will veer towards doing what the flesh desires and end up in a bad place. This is what I believe.

The solution to overcoming the lousy report presented by our flesh is to walk in the Spirit of God and always be attentive to His voice. Prayer and fasting are typically good spiritual practices to keep the fire burning for Jesus! Neh'enah.

23

Though I Walk Through . . .

"The LORD is my shepherd; I shall not want.
He makes me to lie down in green pastures;
He leads me beside the still waters.
He restores my soul;
He leads me in the paths of righteousness
For His name's sake.
Yea, though I walk through the valley of the shadow of death,
I will fear no evil;
For You are with me;
Your rod and Your staff, they comfort me.
You prepare a table before me in the presence of my enemies;
You anoint my head with oil;
My cup runs over.
Surely goodness and mercy shall follow me
All the days of my life;
And I will dwell in the house of the LORD
Forever." (Psalm 23:1)

The power behind every word that comes from God is in the knowledge of knowing Him. If we don't know the Lord in a personal way, our Bible knowledge becomes only intellectual, rendering it powerless to impact us and deliver us.

Too often, you will find a dear brother or sister quoting a memory verse or reciting some powerful portion of God's word, but all to no avail, for the Word of God is not within them but capsulated in the carnal mind at best.

In building a relationship with Christ and getting to know Jesus personally, God's servants will progressively experience raptures of His grace. He will continually be taken up into the third heaven and see His glory and a greater fullness of who Christ is.

Once caught up with Christ, the Word becomes living and powerful, with the megaton power to transform the human soul.

God Made Real!

Let us look at King David and his Psalmist gift.

David would find himself undergoing excruciating tests and trials in his own life, and if you notice carefully, he made songs out of these experiences. The difference between him being tested by circumstances and others is that David knew Jehovah God personally. This made a difference in his life.

David's relationship with God made his testimony real, and his expression through prayer and song was so convincing; his writing ministry transcended and bypassed the natural.

Listening to David sing, worship, and write the Psalms was genuinely experiencing the experience of someone who lived in a different world or dimension. I believe this is precisely what Paul refers to when he so knowingly puts it in his writing to the Galatians and says, "Walk in the Spirit, and you shall not fulfill the lust of the flesh."

You see, memorizing the Word of God by heart is a good thing if you are in a contest of "Who can quote more Scriptures." When living your daily life, the Word of God must become living bread. It will sustain your life through anything that comes your way.

No Power!

A confrontation ensued in one encounter that Jesus had with the Pharisees of His day. Here's the story as Christ unfolded some truth to them: "And the Father Himself, who sent Me, has testified of Me. You have neither heard His voice at any time nor seen His form. But you do not have His word abiding in you, because whom He sent, Him you do not believe. You search the Scriptures, for in them you think you have eternal life; and these are they which testify of Me. But you are not willing to come to Me that you may have life." (John 5:37-40)

The power of God's Word(s) resides within the man who has made Jesus Christ the Lord of his life. If Christ is not the Lord of that man's heart, then you must know that that man has no spiritual power within himself to be or do anything for God.

When King David says, "**The Lord is my shepherd; I shall not want,**" he says with conviction and full assurance that Jehovah is. This wasn't done in words only but in deeds as well. David knew that Jehovah had his life in his hands and was not mimicking anyone else regarding this. With David, it was very personal! He knows God!

End the Struggle!

Often, I hear believers get discouraged because God has not answered their prayers or given a breakthrough for this or that. I'm sure you have listened to people complaining to God for not answering their petitions.

I venture to say that most of what people are complaining about and feel God should do for them was never promised to them. They are mad about something God never told them He would do for them. They may quote Isaiah 53 and claim how His stripes heal us. They may know the Scriptures by memory but don't know the God of the Scriptures. Are you getting this?

Now, why would this happen?

It usually happens because people don't know what David knew. They don't know God!

They may go to church, pay their tithes, and even serve at their local church; however, Jesus is not in their hearts, and therefore, their prayers are coming out of their selfish knowledge and not birthed in the heart of God, which is gained through intimacy in prayer. Neh'enah.

24

Get Out of the House! - Part 1

"And behold, there came a man named Jairus, and he was a ruler of the synagogue. And he fell down at Jesus' feet and begged Him to come to his house, for he had an only daughter about twelve years of age, and she was dying. But as He went, the multitudes thronged Him. Now a woman, having a flow of blood for twelve years, who had spent all her livelihood on physicians and could not be healed by any, came from behind and touched the border of His garment. And immediately her flow of blood stopped." (Luke 8:41-44)

"Now a certain woman had a flow of blood for twelve years, and had suffered many things from many physicians. She had spent all that she had and was no better, but rather grew worse. When she heard about Jesus, she came behind Him in the crowd and touched His garment. For she said, "If only I may touch His clothes, I shall be made well." (Mark 5:25-28)

In this story, as told by the disciples in different gospel books, we will discover how a woman's faith healed her from an infirmity she had held on to for twelve years.

Can you imagine this? For twelve years, this woman had a flow of blood that would not cease. At first, I am sure she thought it was expected; after some weeks, she thought it would be a good idea to go and visit the doctor; after not getting results from one doctor, she went to see another specialist, and so forth. This continued for twelve years. Unbelievable! Like any situation we can't overcome, we get used to it. We begin to make excuses for our lack of how things have turned out, etc. We see this in our health, relationships, marriages, businesses, and families.

Accustomed!

What does accustomed mean? If you're accustomed to something, you're used to it. Being accustomed has to do with habits and lifestyle.

Getting accustomed to something God allowed is one thing; however, getting accustomed to something that fear, doubt, or unbelief has robbed you of is very different.

Today, many in the Christian faith have become accustomed to living and thinking a certain way—all because they couldn't overcome fear, doubt, pride, etc.

Somewhere down the road of struggle and pain, you decided that this was your life and that "things" would always be this way.

Do you understand what I am saying to you today?

Becoming accustomed gives you a particular identity. All too often, people begin to know you by your identity rather than by what God intended for you.

Please understand what I am saying: Leaving an old mindset for a new one is never easy. Everyone would do it if it were, but it is not easy. The Bible says this woman lived in a challenging situation for twelve years.

Let us return to this woman's life and see how the Holy Spirit wants to reveal His heart to us.

Obstacles Inside the House

When reading this story, one's attention is drawn to the woman's need and the miracle that followed. Rarely does anyone speak of the battle within her mind and heart and the steps she had to take to be free.

Somehow, people think that God works like a microwave. If you need hot food, press the bottom! It's tempting to read the Scriptures with this idea and hope that God will fix all our circumstances in 30 seconds. We have all been there.

Let's ponder this quietly: This woman had been bleeding for 12 years; she had probably been living in isolation and was still sick and broke! No family member wanted her near; no synagogue would accept her due to the laws of purification – can you picture this? Can you imagine what is going on in her mind?

The Scripture says that Jesus was passing by, and as He made his way through the streets, she probably heard the crowds. I am sure she knew who Jesus was and what miracles He had performed in the surrounding regions. She probably thought, "I am so glad Jesus is touching and healing people. Good for them!"
- Could He do it for me? Probably not!
- I probably smell bad!
- God has probably punished me, and that is why I am like this!
- No one has come to visit me; why would Jesus visit me?
- Where would I get money if I needed to give Him an offering? I have nothing!
- Doctors already said, "There is nothing we can do!" I'm damned!

The Invitation!

Then something happened! Something deep within her started to arise. It was the faith of God, not her faith, but the faith of God!

The Scripture says, **"If only I may touch His clothes, I shall be made well."**

We don't see God move in our lives partly because of our decisions. God never told us to do certain things; we only assumed He was leading us there. But it wasn't Him; it was our hearts. Our hearts deceived us! You must know this.

The rule is that we wait upon the Lord until He invites us to go, do, and be first. Then, we obey, knowing that the Holy Spirit is leading us.

Once this woman of God recognized the faith of God rising within her, she proceeded to make a move and get out of her house.

One thing we must understand is that the battle is inside. The flesh hates God. It fights God at every turn and never aligns itself with God's will. Breaking out of your flesh [your house] is the first step to victory. Neh'en-ah.

25

Get Out of the House! – Part 2

When she heard about Jesus, she came behind Him in the crowd and touched His garment. For she said, "If only I may touch His clothes, I shall be made well." (Mark 5:25-28)

In studying the woman with the issue of blood, we have seen how her life was impacted negatively by her infirmity and how she battled for 12 years. The Scripture says that she had spent all her livelihood in doctors and wasn't any better. Think of this.

How many people do you know that are living their lives trapped by disease, financial situations, abusive relationships, lousy family ordeals, and failing marriages?

The fact that we live in a fallen world doesn't contribute to the well-being of any of this. Due to man's fallenness and sin's corruption, we need God in our personal walk more than anyone cares to admit. We need the Lord!

As this woman pondered all the commotion on the street, her spirit started to wonder if there might be something in it for her, especially given her circumstances.

What else did she have? She had already lost everything. Things seemed extremely grim until she heard the crowds on the street. What was all that noise, and why were so many people accompanying this man in the middle of the crowd called Jesus?

Now, she had heard about Jesus, but what could He do? As the crowds continued to make noise, she started to feel a stirring in her heart. Her mind pondered all the impossibilities, but her spirit [heart] began to see the possibilities, led by the Lord.

After overcoming those mental battles, she stepped out of the house and into the street.

An experience of God that doesn't cost you anything, won't do anything! Things were about to change for her!

Obstacles Outside the House

As she went out into the crowds and joined them, she said within herself, "For she said, **"If only I may touch His clothes, I shall be made well."**

As this woman overcame her mental fears, embarrassments, and criticisms, she pursued Jesus. She knew something in her heart that others didn't; she was convinced she would be healed if she touched the hem of Jesus' garments. So she went for it!

Perseverance!

Sometimes, we must understand that if the Lord invites our hearts to take a step of faith, we must press on through crowds of people, adversity, opposition, etc.

Our victory truly depends on the invitation. Were we invited or not? We must determine this to see complete victory. If we haven't been invited, don't move from where you are presently.

The most significant battle must first be won in the mind. The second battle is external; if we win the first battle, our perseverance will determine the second one.

This woman had it. Listen to this:

And Jesus said, "Who touched Me?"
When all denied it, Peter and those with him said, "Master, the multitudes throng and press You, and You say, 'Who touched Me?' "
But Jesus said, "Somebody touched Me, for I perceived power going out from Me." Now when the woman saw that she was not hidden, she came trembling; and falling down before Him, she declared to Him in the presence of all the people the reason she had touched Him and how she was healed immediately.
And He said to her, "Daughter, be of good cheer; your faith has made you well. Go in peace." (Luke 8:45-48)

To be a person of spiritual power, one must first learn to listen to God. One must walk in humility and desire to be broken by the Lord. Once you have made this your lifestyle, you are ready to walk with God, as He will use your life to magnify His Name!

Guilty as Charged!

Too often, people are looking for the way out, the way in, healing, a financial miracle, a spiritual breakthrough, or direction for their families, ministries, businesses, etc. As we have learned, bad situations can last weeks, months, and even years.

Believers tend to ask for a miracle and the church to pray for them. I'm not against people getting prayed for, but we must educate people to go to God for themselves and find out precisely what God needs them to do. We lack such practice in the local church, especially in our modern-day Christianity.

We must learn to sit and wait before God until we get invited into what He needs us to do. Once we hear the voice of the Lord, we must persevere to do what we are asked to do.

This is the will of God for every servant of God. Neh'enah.

26

In Entering the New!

"Now the LORD spoke to Moses in the plains of Moab by the Jordan, across from Jericho, saying, "Speak to the children of Israel, and say to them: 'When you have crossed the Jordan into the land of Canaan, then you shall drive out all the inhabitants of the land from before you, destroy all their engraved stones, destroy all their molded images, and demolish all their high places; you shall dispossess the inhabitants of the land and dwell in it, for I have given you the land to possess. And you shall divide the land by lot as an inheritance among your families; to the larger you shall give a larger inheritance, and to the smaller you shall give a smaller inheritance; there everyone's inheritance shall be whatever falls to him by lot. You shall inherit according to the tribes of your fathers. But if you do not drive out the inhabitants of the land from before you, then it shall be that those whom you let remain shall be irritants in your eyes and thorns in your sides, and they shall harass you in the land where you dwell. Moreover it shall be that I will do to you as I thought to do to them.'" (Numbers 33:50-56)

We often prepare for the New Year before we enter it on our calendar. We evaluate our previous year, our gains and losses, the things we left out that could have been done, etc.

Along with this mindset, we organize our personal and professional lives. We plan for the upcoming months and position ourselves for a more prosperous year. We have all done this.

A New Horizon

The children of Israel were coming to the end of forty years of living in the desert. They were positioned to enter something new—something promised, yes, something that would require a higher level of responsibility and commitment.

If you have been walking with God for some time, you would know that God always instructs His people to do certain things as they press forward. God always gives direction and provides the resources to carry out His orders.

In the story above, Moses had received God's instruction on what the people of Israel would do when the time came to cross over the River Jordan and into the promised Land.

A quick note here is that just because it is called the Promised Land, it doesn't mean life will be easy. It doesn't mean there won't be any challenges, tests, trials, etc.

The First Set of Instructions

"'When you have crossed the Jordan into the land of Canaan, then you shall drive out all the inhabitants of the land from before you, destroy all their engraved stones, destroy all their molded images, and demolish all their high places; you shall dispossess the inhabitants of the land and dwell in it, for I have given you the land to possess.'" (Numbers 33:51-53)

As soon as you entered this new opportunity, a new position, a new venture, the children of Israel were ordered to drive out all the inhabitants of the land. Not just some but all. This would not be easy for so many reasons, but not impossible. If the Lord orders us to do anything, we would be better off obeying than fighting Him.

Sometimes, it seems God allows us to get away with things in our walk. Not that He does, but it seems that way. I'm unsure if He looks at us and knows that we are immature in so many ways, but as we grow in Him, He begins to teach us to adjust things that need to be adjusted. We can do this through pure obedience, or we will do it through regrets and the consequences of our rebellion.

As the Lord presses the issue into the heart and mind of Moses, He adds, **"destroy all their engraved stones, destroy all their molded images, and demolish all their high places..."** When I read the words destroy and demolish, I can almost tell God's emotions and true feelings over the idolatry afforded to other false gods. He hated it!

God desired that His people would move into a land that would be theirs as promised but had to do some work – they would have to demolish and destroy things those other inhabitants used to worship their false gods.

There might be things in our hearts that God has been dealing with for some time, but this time around, they seem a bit more serious. It almost feels like God will not tolerate our foolishness and will judge us.

Part of possessing fully something promised has to do with making room for God to have His way. If we have idolatry in our hearts or made altars for something other than Him, we divide our hearts and desires between two gods. This will not work as we enter the land and possess our territory.

Second Set of Instructions

"And you shall divide the land by lot as an inheritance among your families; to the larger you shall give a larger inheritance, and to the smaller you shall give a smaller inheritance; there everyone's inheritance shall be whatever falls to him by lot. You shall inherit according to the tribes of your fathers. "

If we obey the first set of instructions, we can move into the land and divide it into lots. What does this mean for you and me?

This means that God will give you a sphere to work with, an area where you and I can grow. It may be big, or the lot may be small; the only thing to remember is that God gives according to His grace.

Just like spiritual gifts, God gives them according to His grace. **"Having then gifts differing according to the grace that is given to us..."** (Romans 12:6) or 1 Corinthians 12:11 reads, **"But one and the same Spirit works all these things, distributing to each one individually as He wills."**

If we prove ourselves faithful with the little we initially received, the Lord may promote and give us more. **"If you are faithful in little things, you will be faithful in large ones."** (Luke 16:10)

As we begin to display our gratitude for receiving a lot, we cultivate it and produce fruit for the glory of God. This is how we advance in God's kingdom. We show ourselves faithful and responsible with all that God gives us. We can't lose that feeling of gratitude for all God has provided us.

Consequence of Not Following Instructions

"But if you do not drive out the inhabitants of the land from before you, then it shall be that those whom you let remain shall be irritants in your eyes and thorns in your sides, and they shall harass you in the land where you dwell."

What impresses me more and more is how believers today get so excited about something one day and then do the opposite the next day.

The Lord's instructions to Moses and the children of Israel were comprehensive. He didn't leave any room for guessing. He told them precisely what to do in this new realm; everything depended on their obedience.

If the children of Israel didn't obey His instructions, the consequences of their disobedience would rapidly come upon them. **"...then it shall be that those whom you let remain shall be irritants in your eyes and thorns in your sides..."**

Think of this: Isn't this what happens when we are asked to take some action against our wrongdoing, and we disobey; do you remember how painful this is? How many of us have lived this experience?

A quick way to abort or annul what God has intended to be a blessing for us is to disobey Him, especially in things He talks explicitly to us about.

May God help us to be quick to listen and obey Him as we enter a new realm or dimension of His love and calling for us. Neh'enah.

27

Roots!

"Either make the tree good and its fruit good, or else make the tree bad and its fruit bad; for a tree is known by its fruit." (Matthew 12:33)

"If the dough offered as first fruits is holy, so is the whole lump, and if the root is holy, so are the branches." (Romans 11:16)

It was an early Thursday morning as I made my way through my prayer walk, and the Holy Spirit quickened my heart with these words: *"Have you considered the roots?"* "Roots?" I questioned. The Holy Spirit assured me and said, *"Yes, roots. If the roots of a tree are bad, the fruit of the tree will be bad!"*

I pondered why the Holy Spirit would want to converse on such a topic.

As I kept on walking and praying, the voice of God began to teach me about "the why" people are hardly ever delivered from demonic oppressions and possessions. The "why" believers are robbed of their destinies in God and why full potential is ever fully discovered.

Still Bound!

While having lunch with a pastor friend, the pastor shared with me a dear brother who had attended their church for some time but then stopped.

After being months away from church, the brother stopped by for a visit during a midweek service. Prayer was being offered for all, and when he was asked if he needed prayer, he answered, "No!" The pastor then asked, "Why not?" The brother proceeded to say, "Nothing ever changes for me! I'm so tired of all this. I'm frustrated and feel that nothing changes for me." In hearing this, I knew the brother wasn't lying.

Why is it that attending church has become such a powerless experience for so many? I have heard this same story for years. Is it a church problem? Is it the people's problem? It's somebody's problem of why people are not finding freedom and a more excellent experience in the presence of God. Yes, but who is at fault?

While I was meditating on the situation, the Holy Spirit began to clarify some things for me. He showed me that people remain in the same state due to their old roots, which have never been redeemed. Yes, prayers have been made by both the pastor and the one receiving the prayer; however, the prayer was not made from the heart but from the mind, and yes, this is my humble opinion. Old roots were not cut, removed, or washed by the powerful blood of Jesus!

Everything Starts with the Quickening Spirit!

The Holy Spirit is a quickening Spirit that will awaken the consciousness of the lost sinner. It is the only way to come to God if the Spirit draws Him. "**No one is able to come to Me unless the Father Who sent Me attracts and draws him and gives him the desire to come to Me, and** [then] **I will raise him up** [from the dead] **at the last day.**" (John 6:44 -Amplified Version)

Many who come to our churches with needs, pain, a broken heart, or an illness expect to be healed. Some do, and some don't. Whatever the outcome of the church gathering, most didn't come out redeemed from a life of sin and corruption. They made prayers but with no real connection to God. Some felt better because of all the adrenaline and prayers exchanged, but the heart was left untouched!

Unless God has touched the heart through an invitation to come and repent of all sin – that heart will be unchanged! That man or woman will go home the same way they came. This is sad, very sad.

The Scripture in Romans 11:16 says, **"And if the root is holy, so are the branches."**

Unless there has been a thorough cleansing of the blood penetrating that selfish heart, one can't be holy. The roots must be holy so the branches can be holy; good fruit will follow this.

If the evidence of righteousness, peace, and joy in the Holy Spirit is not evident, then the kingdom of God has not arrived at that heart. **"For the kingdom of God is not a matter of eating and drinking but of righteousness and peace and joy in the Holy Spirit."** (Romans 14:17 -ESV)

Let us not fool ourselves. Repetitious prayers, songs, and all the liturgy in the world can't save a dying soul any more than an ant can stop a train coming down a mountain. We need the Holy Ghost to intervene in the human heart!

Is the Holy Ghost In the House?

If the Holy Spirit is present, that man or woman will be invited to come and crucify their sinful life once and for all. When the old roots have been cut off and done away with, all the hate, sin, affliction, selfishness, pride, and arrogance will disappear, and that dear man or woman will have holy roots, and the joy of the Lord will finally be their strength! Neh'enah.

28

Overcoming Darkness!

I came across an interesting excerpt while reading a book about overcoming negative mindsets and other influences that hinder our lives a while back.

As I continued reading this article, I came across a story that I would like to share with you in this devotion.

The Two Arrows!

The author says that when life hits us with a crisis, we feel two arrows piercing us through...

The first arrow causes pain externally. We feel immediate discomfort and excruciating pain, which will subside if we take care of it.

The second arrow is the one that causes pain internally. This pain is the one that lingers on and on. Sometimes, this pain will often last days, weeks, months, and even years.

The article sheds much light on what God wants to do with our internal or external pain.
Recognizing Darkness

The second arrow is what hurts people deeper and longer. A trauma of any kind must be healed so that nothing festers in the future and brings that person under any sort of bondage.

Too often, people who experience rough upbringings, a mesmerizing experience when they were young, such as parents fighting or a drunken father or mother, perhaps a storm or fire that burned down your house, all these have the potential to leave deep emotional marks on someone.

In assuming that there is an emotional wound caused by a trauma of some sort, in the natural, one can deal with it psychologically. Compartmentalizing their thoughts and releasing them mentally sometimes helps deal with extreme trauma, but this isn't always the case.

In the spiritual realm, the enemy of our souls, for lack of better terms, is forever attempting to trap God's creation in darkness. It is the enemy's favorite tool to use - pure darkness.

Perhaps you might remember a trauma you experienced as a young child: You might have seen a forest fire, and that scared you so profoundly that it left an indelible mark on you. From that point forward, you go into a panic frenzy every time you see a fire. Do you get me?

This is not a typical or common way to live; this is not God's will for anyone! One might try to convince themselves that it is "ok" and will soon pass. But truthfully, this is not part of God's eternal plan for any of His children.

Overcoming Darkness!

Let us see how darkness must be dealt with, especially the one that has kept us in bondage for a long time.

In Psalm 23, David wrote about his encounter with valleys and shadows of death. It doesn't get darker than that. Here's David, a man after God's own heart, going through a trial of trials. And if you have studied even a bit of David's life, you will wonder, how can a man after God's own heart be going through so much in his lifetime?

David's life testifies that even those highly favored of God will go through the fire of affliction and be tested severely in every way possible.

Listen to the first part of Psalm 23:

"The LORD is my shepherd; I shall not want.
He makes me to lie down in green pastures;
He leads me beside the still waters.
He restores my soul;
He leads me in the path of righteousness
For His name's sake.
Yea, though I walk through the valley of the shadow of death,
I will fear no evil;
For You are with me..." (Psalm 23:1-4)

In this Psalm, David shows us the goodness of God's heart as a Shepherd. He mentions the shepherd's care and concern for his sheep, both in good times and in bad.

David compares himself to a sheep and states that Jehovah is his shepherd. He does not need anything else!

In times of darkness, David reiterates God's faithfulness by saying, "I will fear no evil, for You are with me!" Dwell on that for a bit.

David overcame darkness because Jehovah, who is Light, was with him! Does this make any sense to you? It does to me.

The Truth Regarding Darkness!

"In Him was life, and the life was the light of men." (John 1:4)

Darkness hates the light! It can't stand against it. All the light must do is show up, and the light disappears. It is like this in the natural and much more in the spiritual. Darkness will not and cannot defeat the light. Period. As soon as light appears, darkness disappears!

Thinking that darkness moves so swiftly and cannot be removed from a person or situation is a lie. If you believe that darkness is more powerful than light, you have been fooled by it.
To the believer, I say, "God has put a light inside you. That Light within you is Jesus Himself. That light is like a burning torch of His love. Darkness cannot withstand it, much less overcome it!" The question here is, "Do you, yourself, believe it to be so?"

You see, His life is your Light! He lives within your very being!

Darkness Reacts to Your Every Step!

David believed that God was light and that as he faced the valley and the shadows of death, he felt that with every step he took forward, the light that accompanied him would brighten his path. With every step, the light would advance. Now, if David didn't take a step, neither would the light. Only as we step into the darkness is it pushed back. The darkness will not respond if no light can chase it away.

Look at this word in 1 John 1:5, **"This is the message which we have heard from Him and declare to you, that God is light and in Him is no darkness at all."**

With every step in God, the darkness must obey and step back. Not if it will or maybe it will – no sir, the darkness will have to leave because Jesus the King, the Light of the world, is coming through! Neh'enah.

29

Living Under the Promise!

"For the land which you go to possess is not like the land of Egypt from which you have come, where you sowed your seed and watered it by foot, as a vegetable garden; but the land which you cross over to possess is a land of hills and valleys, which drinks water from the rain of heaven, a land for which the LORD your God cares; the eyes of the LORD your God are always on it, from the beginning of the year to the very end of the year." (Deuteronomy 11:9-12)

God's people were the most blessed creatures on the planet being that Jehovah God was upon them. He created the nation that would follow Him and be expressions of His nature on earth. There were no other peoples on the earth like the Hebrew children.

The hand of God was upon them and would always be with them so long as they followed His lead. It is the same with us.

Choices!

Walking and living our life under the direction of the Holy Spirit, our lives are blessed in such a way – a special way. Every believer who has pledged allegiance to Christ knows exactly what I am talking about.
As choices are made to follow Christ and His commands, there exists a price to be paid for doing this. Living for Jesus is a willful choice that one makes daily. Jesus said, **"If you want to follow Me, you must deny yourself, carry your cross, and follow."**

Nothing happens in a believer's life apart from the will of God. Allow me to emphasize: Many things happen in a person's life, but are those actions carried under the will of God? This is the question.

I venture to say that most of the "good deeds," done in Jesus' Name are nothing more than some type of appeasement to a guilty conscience. People are always doing things to help people, but is this what Jesus has called them to do?

So-called believers do many good works in His Name, but do they have a relationship with Christ? You see Christianity is about a relationship with God, not about how many good deeds you can do with your hands. We must get this once and for all.

Living Under Our Idea of a Promise!

In pondering this truth that I am about to share with you, I realized that the believers in the days of Moses not only had choices to make, but they believed that they were chosen by mere lineage and that there was no need to make any choices.

There are so many Christians today who feel the same way. They have no living relationship with Jesus, but they go to church. They even take a Bible with them, sing the songs, and give offerings. Yet, their lives are not changed! They are still drunkards, womanizers, cheaters, and thieves.

They like the Christian culture, but they are not willing to be changed by it. Perhaps, if Christianity fits their lifestyle, they might embrace a little bit of it, but not at the expense of surrendering their life to Christ.

As the children of Israel lived "for God," they had to continue watering their fields, growing their crops, and working hard at making life happen. Do you know how tiring this lifestyle is? Day in and day out, God's people labored on the side of the desert.

Living Under God's Promise.

Things could have changed for them forty years before, but they refused to enter the Promised Land. They didn't have the faith to trust Jehovah and thus forfeited what God had in store.

The promise was that **"the land which you cross over to possess is a land of hills and valleys, which drinks water from the rain of heaven, a land for which the LORD your God cares; the eyes of the LORD your God are always on it, from the beginning of the year to the very end of the year."**

In the Promised Land, the difference would be that God would supernaturally care for them. God promised to rain upon it. Rain was the difference. God cared for His promise; God will always take care of what He initiates. He would care for it; His eyes would be upon it from the beginning of the year till the end of it. What a guarantee!

Living Under His Direction

As we allow the Holy Spirit to direct our lives, we will always come across His promises. Those promises are contingent upon our choices. If the Lord initiates an idea, and we follow through with it, know that the Lord's eyes will be upon it. If the Lord is not the One directing us into something, we might as well forget God's favor to rest upon us.

Too many people are running their "own personal show." God is not required to bless or be part of anything we initiate. We must get this truth and let it go deep into our hearts. Most people, as I said before, live for themselves, not for Jesus, and it doesn't matter what church you attend! Neh'enah.

30

Jesus, the Glory of God!

"For it is the God who commanded light to shine out of darkness, who has shone in our hearts to give the light of the knowledge of the glory of God in the face of Jesus Christ." (2 Corinthians 4:6)

"And the Word (Christ) became flesh (human, incarnate) and tabernacled (fixed His tent of flesh, lived awhile) among us; and we [actually] saw His glory (His honor, His majesty), such glory as an only begotten son receives from his father, full of grace (favor, loving-kindness) and truth." (John 1:14 -Amplified Version)

"Jesus replied, "Have I been with you for so long, and you have not known me, Philip? The person who has seen me has seen the Father! How can you say, 'Show us the Father'? Do you not believe that I am in the Father, and the Father is in me? The words that I say to you, I do not speak on my own initiative, but the Father residing in me performs his miraculous deeds. Believe me that I am in the Father, and the Father is in me, but if you do not believe me, believe because of the miraculous deeds themselves. I tell you the solemn truth, the person who believes in me will perform the miraculous deeds that I am doing, and will perform greater deeds than these, because I am going to the Father. And I will do whatever you ask in my name so that the Father may be glorified in the Son. If you ask me anything in my name, I will do it." (John 14:9-14 -Today's English Version)

He is the image of the invisible God, the firstborn over all creation. For by Him all things were created that are in heaven and that are on earth, visible and invisible, whether thrones or dominions or principalities or powers. All things were created through Him and for Him. And He is before all things, and in Him all things consist. And He is the head of the body, the church, who is the beginning, the firstborn from the dead, that in all things He may have the preeminence. For it pleased the Father that in Him all the fullness should dwell." (Colossians 1:6-9)

Reading the above Scriptures, I realized God's glory is found in Jesus' face. We must see Christ as God's glory and not as some "god" who exists only to give us all our wants. Too often, Christ has become just that!

Many believers today have made Jesus an idol, a type of doctor, or Santa Claus; yes, someone who exists only to meet some need. This type of thinking is fleshly at best and gives off the wrong idea about who God really is.

Though God may heal your disease or sickness or bring about much-needed deliverance, this is not the only reason Jesus came to Earth. He came to reveal our heavenly Father, to exemplify who the Father was, and to show how all creation was called to come back and worship the King of Glory!

When Jesus walked the earth, He was full of grace and power. Perhaps people around Him never realized what was inside of Him, but God was in Him. As He moved from town to town, He dispersed God's glory everywhere He went.

It is no wonder that people saw Him differently, or that when speaking in open-air meetings, people knew that this man was not like other religious advocates. Jesus thought differently, communicated differently, and acted differently. Authority and power were manifested through Him, making negating that God's glory was present even more challenging!

Now, this very Jesus performed many signs and wonders while on Earth. Through His ministry, many experienced God in a very tangible way. Some were healed of incurable diseases. Others were delivered from demonic oppression and possession. All this was done in the open for all the world to see. To amplify even further the power of God, some were resurrected from their dead state and brought to life again. What did this? It was the glory of God moving mightily through the hands of Jesus!

Seeing the Father!

In John 14, Jesus replied to Philip, **"Have I been with you for so long, and you have not known me, Philip? The person who has seen me has seen the Father! How can you say, 'Show us the Father'?"**

Another verse says, **"He is the image of the invisible God."** To see Jesus is to see the Father. Jesus exemplified the character and nature of our heavenly Father as He walked the earth. Jesus was not trying to be good; He epitomized goodness. He wasn't trying to be loving; He was love. To see Christ is to see the Father.

Also, know that it takes faith to see God. I will always believe this. Metaphysically or psychologically, it is not enough to convince ourselves. I genuinely believe that unless God opens our eyes, we won't see the works of God, especially the work wrought in Christ by God through the power of the Holy Spirit.

Seeing the Father in Christ must be a work of faith. The Holy Spirit must unveil this mystery to the spirit of man, his inner man. You see, once this happens in the center of man's spirit, nothing will be impossible for him or her.

The Fullness of God Dwells in Jesus!

"For it pleased the Father that in Him all the fullness should dwell." Everything that the Father is, has been deposited into Jesus Christ our Lord. When we see Jesus, we experience the Father, all of Him. We experience His love, embrace, mercy, forgiveness, adoption, etc.

To know Jesus is to know the glory of God. If we see His glory, we won't want anything else!

As I close this meditation, I want you to know that the cultivation of this glory of God in our lives is a must. It's not automatic; it must be cultivated and guarded from fleshly desires and selfish passions. The flesh always wants death; we don't see it that way, but it does! Remember, the flesh can only sin, and it can only produce corruption.

If we neglect this cultivation of the glory of God in us, we will end up surrounded and enslaved by earthly idols. Cultivate His glory in you, I say! Neh'enah.

31

Recognizing the Glory of God!

"But as He went, the multitudes thronged Him. Now a woman, having a flow of blood for twelve years, who had spent all her livelihood on physicians and could not be healed by any, came from behind and touched the border of His garment. And immediately her flow of blood stopped. And Jesus said, "Who touched Me?" When all denied it, Peter and those with him said, "Master, the multitudes throng and press You, and You say, 'Who touched Me?' "But Jesus said, "Somebody touched Me, for I perceived power going out from Me." Now when the woman saw that she was not hidden, she came trembling; and falling down before Him, she declared to Him in the presence of all the people the reason she had touched Him and how she was healed immediately. And He said to her, "Daughter, be of good cheer; your faith has made you well. Go in peace." (Luke 8:42-48)

In recognizing God's glory, one must be able to see this with the eye of the spirit, not with one's intellectual sense. Many have made decisions based upon a feeling, or simply put, they were moved by what they understood with their common sense. This usually has no effect and fails to produce any results.

Now, there are natural results that build up a natural reservoir and spiritual results that fill up our spiritual lives. Whoever dominates your life, whether flesh or spirit, will fill your life.

Could Not Be Healed by Any!

In our story above, we find a woman who had had a blood issue for about 12 years. This was a long time ago, and no one could do anything to fix it. The professionals of her day had given up, not to mention that all her money was used up in medical expenses, but unfortunately, there was no cure.

After trying and trying, there was nothing to show for her effort. This is not an uncommon story to any of us, as we have all been touched by this woman's infirmity. We have all attempted to fix many things in our lives without seeing a breakthrough for weeks, months, and even years!

How Many Times?

My thoughts of this woman go back to what made her come out of her living place when she heard all the people passing by? What motivated her to literally step out of her house and join the procession of all those following Jesus for different interests?

Had Jesus passed by her house at other times? I'm not sure, but how many times have we missed out on God's grace and power all because we considered other people's opinions and criticisms?

Have you ever considered why some of our lives are stifled or paralyzed by fear, and what others think of us?

Now, this woman knew that she was not allowed to come close to people due to her illness, but this didn't hold her down or hold her back. She saw something.

She Saw the Glory of God!

As this woman saw the glory of God in the face of Jesus, something so deep in her said, "Today is your day of salvation! Get up! Go!" As she made her way to the crowd, she probably thought to herself, "I am not worthy to see God's face, for I am a sinner, and God has punished me with this issue of blood. I will go through the back door and touch the hem of

His garment only! No one will see me or feel me."

The woman made her way and touched the hem, and to her amazement, Jesus said, "Who touched Me?" Peter said to Jesus, "Everyone has been touching you. Jesus, what do you mean that someone touched you?" Jesus continued to press for information and said, "**Somebody touched Me, for I perceived power going out from Me.**"

Interestingly, none of the people who touched him during this procession brought this crowd to a stop or made Jesus stop. Why not? If I could make a bet, I assure you that not everyone there touched Jesus with faith. They had not seen the glory of God in the face of Jesus! They were following other interests.

The Woman Explains Herself!

"Now, when the woman saw that she was not hidden, she came trembling; and falling down before Him, she declared to Him in the presence of all the people the reason she had touched Him and how she was healed immediately. And He said to her, "Daughter, be of good cheer; your faith has made you well. Go in peace."

After the woman unveils her motives, Jesus said to her, "**Daughter, be of good cheer; your faith has made you well. Go in peace.**"

I believe that God sees those who see Him. When someone acknowledges God's glory on Jesus's face, they will undoubtedly receive what they came for. To God be the glory now and always! Neh'enah.

32

Contact with the Glory of God!

"And I, Daniel, alone saw the vision, for the men who were with me did not see the vision; but a great terror fell upon them, so that they fled to hide themselves. Therefore I was left alone when I saw this great vision, and no strength remained in me; for my vigor was turned to frailty in me, and I retained no strength. Yet I heard the sound of his words; and while I heard the sound of his words I was in a deep sleep on my face, with my face to the ground. Suddenly, a hand touched me, which made me tremble on my knees and on the palms of my hands. And he said to me, "O Daniel, man greatly beloved, understand the words that I speak to you, and stand upright, for I have now been sent to you." While he was speaking this word to me, I stood trembling. Then he said to me, "Do not fear, Daniel, for from the first day that you set your heart to understand, and to humble yourself before your God, your words were heard; and I have come because of your words." (Daniel 10:7-10)

If there is something I have learned about God's glory, it is this: God's glory doesn't depend upon my emotional state to come down and empower my life. God's glory is a work of God's grace upon those who believe.

I know that in many meetings today, churches try to set up the ambience by dimming the lights, setting up the stage, and playing songs that I call flesh-movers. You know what I mean: First, the first five dancing praise songs and then the last three tearjerkers. Sounds funny, but I'm not trying to be.

Many believe this is necessary to experience God in a deep and mystical way. Still, I wholeheartedly believe that if a man or woman will humble themselves, God will come and visit such a person and touch them with glorious power. God's glory is a matter of the heart, not a matter of the art.

Daniel Alone Saw the Vision!

The Scripture above says that Daniel was alone when God visited him. I have seen this pattern in men and women who have pledged their devotion and loyalty to God. What makes these experiences so special is that there is no hype surrounding them. There is no public setting, and God will touch a man who has set himself apart for His purposes.

The interesting point here is that Daniel was surrounded by several men who happened to flee when Daniel was visited by God. It says that great terror fell on them, and they took off.

You see, God always sets his servants apart from everything that surrounds them so that He may have a private time to speak to them. This is such a holy time.

Left Powerless!

When Daniel was left alone, and all those with him took off, God began to visit him.

Now, the Scripture goes on to note these experiences – let us look at them:

"Therefore I was left alone when I saw this great vision, and no strength remained in me; for my vigor was turned to frailty in me, and I retained no strength. Yet I heard the sound of his words; and while I heard the sound of his words I was in a deep sleep on my face, with my face to the ground."

The first thing that happens when one experiences God is the weakening of all one knew or adhered to. God will begin an emptying process.

This emptying process has to do with fleshly strength being removed. God doesn't need anyone strong, or able, or established. He needs someone willing to hear and obey! I believe that many believe that their prayer of salvation has brought them in, so there is no need to pursue anything else. This is one of the biggest lies the enemy tells believers today. "You don't need more; you don't need to sacrifice; you don't need to follow godly authority..."

People get so caught up in themselves that they forget the One who gave them life.

Vigor for Frailty

An interesting take here is this one: vigor exchanged for frailty. It was the Lord's will to bring Daniel to a point where he would have to reach a "zero point" in his life.

People who are vigorous, zealous, and always talk a big game are usually the worst at following through with what God has for them. They are all talk but no action! You also have those who all they want is to learn but never come to the knowledge of the truth.

When God calls a man or a woman to do His bidding, they usually realize that they are not worthy to be called His servants. They are afraid to take steps of faith, and they typically shy away from any commission God might call them to.

When a servant realizes that in them there is no power to carry out God's commission, this is usually the time when God visits them with a touch of His glory. God is not interested in how much you know, but how much of what you know you practice daily.

As we read on, we realize that God's touch upon Daniel's head sent him to his face and knocked him out. Unless you get knocked out by the Lord, your faculties will not experience a change.

After Daniel is touched by God and awakened from the vision, he is trembling and shaking.

Church, these are characteristics of someone who has been touched by God. They are a sure sign of someone who has come in contact with His glory.

As I close this devotion, I want to challenge your heart to pursue God in this manner. Don't be content with where you presently are. There is so much more for you and me. Let us press in until we are clothed with power from on high. Neh'enah.

33

Transformed by His Voice!

"On the same day Jesus went out of the house and sat by the sea. And great multitudes were gathered together to Him, so that He got into a boat and sat; and the whole multitude stood on the shore.
Then He spoke many things to them in parables, saying: "Behold, a sower went out to sow. And as he sowed, some seed fell by the wayside; and the birds came and devoured them. Some fell on stony places, where they did not have much earth; and they immediately sprang up because they had no depth of earth. But when the sun was up they were scorched, and because they had no root they withered away. And some fell among thorns, and the thorns sprang up and choked them. But others fell on good ground and yielded a crop: some a hundredfold, some sixty, some thirty. He who has ears to hear, let him hear!"
And the disciples came and said to Him, "Why do You speak to them in parables?"
He answered and said to them, "Because it has been given to you to know the mysteries of the kingdom of heaven, but to them it has not been given. For whoever has, to him more will be given, and he will have abundance; but whoever does not have, even what he has will be taken away from him. Therefore I speak to them in parables, because seeing they do not see, and hearing they do not hear, nor do they understand. And in them the prophecy of Isaiah is fulfilled, which says:
'Hearing you will hear and shall not understand,
And seeing you will see and not perceive;
For the hearts of this people have grown dull.
Their ears are hard of hearing,
And their eyes they have closed,
Lest they should see with their eyes and hear with their ears,
Lest they should understand with their hearts and turn,

So that I should heal them.'
But blessed are your eyes for they see, and your ears for they hear; for assuredly, I say to you that many prophets and righteous men desired to see what you see, and did not see it, and to hear what you hear, and did not hear it." (Matthew 13:1-17)

In our journey with Jesus, we can find seasons when God's voice is clear to hear, and our hearts quickly capture His will. There were times when we couldn't wait for God to unveil His will in tangible ways so that we would run and obey all of it!

The desire to please God was at an all-time high, and obedience to His will and ways was always our priority. These are seasons of great accomplishment and advancement for our life and His kingdom.

These seasons of significant advancement are genuinely remarkable. They leave an indelible mark in our hearts as a testimony of God's power flowing in and through us. We all must desire to live this type of life for God!

Challenging Times!

Now, along with the seasons of significant advancement, we also encounter seasons of incredible dullness, dryness, and emptiness. These seasons come upon us due to various reasons.

There are times of disillusionment, unfulfilled expectations, heartbreak, disappointment- whether caused by oneself or others- and a profound sense of failure.

Because of these mental and emotional obstacles, one often loses sight of God's presence, making it increasingly difficult to hear and see Him move within us. Consequently, after wandering in this "desert," one may find oneself spiritually deaf and blind.

The Value of Hearing His Voice

For our lives to discover joy and peace in God's will, we must allow the Holy Spirit to guide us in His ways – God's ways. Nothing pleases God more than when His creation fulfills its purpose!

Only in the center of God's will can a person find true peace and joy. When a servant of God allows the Holy Spirit to lead them, divine order becomes inevitable. God will direct their steps according to His pattern and design. It has been said that tranquility is the fruit of an ordered mind. When our minds are aligned and submitted to God's design, we will experience peace within, reflecting His glory in our lives.

Nothing is more heartbreaking, in my opinion than attending a church meeting or Bible study and completely missing God's original intent for bringing you there. The chance to be transformed more into His image and missing it due to passive rebellion or failing to engage with Him with a heart of worship is truly a shame. I am confident in my words; I have encountered this unfortunate situation frequently.

Where is the Change?

I have often heard people say that some Christians are not really all they say they are.

They criticize and poke fun at church-going believers because they fail to keep their testimony of a new life in Christ, and there is no visible transformation. I am sure you have experienced this yourself.

But why is there no transformation?

Let me outline some actions that God's servants typically take when they hear His voice, and I will also explain why there is often no change or transformation in a so-called Christian believer.

When the word of the Lord is preached, taught, or shared in any forum, the servant of God will hear it with his natural ears while seeing the man or woman of God prophesy it. At this time, the hearer will do one or two of the following:
1. He will hear but not understand what the Spirit is saying.
2. He will listen to but only understand part or half of what the Spirit says through the Word.
3. He will hear but ignore what was imparted.
4. He will listen but willfully rebel against God's order.
5. He will hear and obey! This brings about transformation and likeness to Christ.

As I conclude this meditation today, I encourage you to sit at Jesus's feet. Establish a daily practice of waiting for a response. This is how a genuine relationship with God is cultivated and brings about transformation. Neh'enah.

34

The Beauty of Hearing God's Voice!

"Now, when they had gone through Phrygia and the region of Galatia, they were forbidden by the Holy Spirit to preach the word in Asia. After they had come to Mysia, they tried to go into Bithynia, but the Spirit did not permit them. So passing by Mysia, they came down to Troas. And a vision appeared to Paul in the night. A man of Macedonia stood and pleaded with him, saying, "Come over to Macedonia and help us." Now after he had seen the vision, immediately we sought to go to Macedonia, concluding that the Lord had called us to preach the gospel to them." (Acts 16:6-10)

Years ago, I came across a great book by A.W. Tozer titled God Tells the Man Who Cares. The title emphasizes the importance of knowing God in such intimate ways that one often learns to inquire of the Lord.

How often should a person talk to God? In other words, how much time should an individual spend alone with God in prayer? The answer will vary.

When asked this specific question, many will give an answer that enhances their belief in Christ. No one wants to feel less comfortable in personal prayer even though they don't have an intimate walk or prayer life. So, they will give general answers, such as, "I pray all the time," "I pray when I have my meals," "I pray when I am in need," etc. I am sure you have heard this from dear believers before.

How Deep Is Your Love for Christ?

A genuine and growing relationship with Christ is birthed in the spirit of man by the Holy Spirit. Only the Spirit of God can draw you into a greater fullness of Christ.

As we give ourselves to the Holy Spirit's leadership and promptings, He brings us into a dimension where we can position ourselves and find greater revelation of His will for us.

When we speak of the beauty of hearing His voice, we are talking about being positioned to listen to what the Lord has for us in a profound, personal way.

Listen to this word: **"Jesus answered, 'If anyone [really] loves Me, he will keep My word (teaching); and My Father will love him, and We will come to him and make Our dwelling place with him..."** (John 14:23 -Amplified Version)

When you listen to Jesus saying, **"If anyone [really] loves Me, he will keep My word [teaching]...".** I want you to notice the chain of events that follow in a loving and ever-growing relationship with Jesus. Then He adds, **"and My Father will love him, and We will come to him and make Our dwelling place with him."** Can you see this?

God's Voice Brings Alignment to Us!

In our pursuit of God, the Holy Spirit intends to bring us to a place where we will please the Lord, experience the advancement of His kingdom, and produce fruit. This is how God gets glory!

God's voice always serves God's interest by providing leadership.

The Apostle Paul was a man of great passion and fervor. His heart was aligned with God, and his mind was focused on the Great Commission (Matthew 28:18, 19).

Paul understood that he only had one life to live and that playing games, giving himself to criticism, or even fearing death itself was not an option. He was to press on until the glory of the Lord filled the earth as the waters covered the sea.

Forbidden!

As Paul journeyed through the region of Galatia, he thought it would be a great idea to "preach the word in Asia." Why not? After all, those people needed to hear the message of the kingdom. It made perfect sense to stop there.

However, the Holy Spirit did not allow it! The Scripture says, **"They were forbidden by the Holy Spirit."** The word forbidden means to hinder, forbid, or restrain.

Have you ever been to a place where you felt that it was a great idea to do this or that, and something inside of you said, "No? Don't do it!" Just because something is a great idea doesn't mean God thinks the same way. How many errors have we committed by thinking that something was a great thing, and it turned out to be the worst thing ever?

Then it happened again: **"They tried to go into Bithynia, but the Spirit did not permit them."** This is Holy Spirit leadership!

Many would say, "What is this? Why is God not allowing me to carry out this great idea, plan, or ambition? It is for His kingdom!" Here's where you discover who leads your life: you or the Spirit of God.

Until a Vision from God Comes!

"And a vision appeared to Paul in the night. A man of Macedonia stood and pleaded with him, saying, "Come over to Macedonia and help us."

Now after he had seen the vision, immediately we sought to go to Macedonia, concluding that the Lord had called us to preach the gospel to them."

Any true disciple of Jesus must not go anywhere or do anything without God's approval. In Matthew 6:33, Jesus said, **"Seek first the kingdom of God and all His righteousness...and all these things shall be added unto you."** Paul understood this kingdom principle.

Paul lived a life of submission to God, and his love for Jesus was out of this world. He wouldn't cross any lines, knowing that God would disapprove. We must learn this.

How God Speaks to Us.

His Word. In reading the Bible, the Word of God, everything that has to do with our life has been revealed in His holy Word. To be a born-again believer and not be a student of God's Word is spiritual suicide. Your life will never grow past your knowledge of God's Word.

His Spirit. The relationship we develop and cultivate with the Holy Spirit must be prioritized. "The Spirit of God reveals God's heart to us, for the Spirit of God is the mind of God. But God has revealed them to us through His Spirit. For the Spirit searches all things, yes, the deep things of God. For what man knows the things of a man except the spirit of the man which is in him? Even so no one knows the things of God except the Spirit of God." (1 Corinthians 2:10, 11)

Dreams and Visions. There is much to say about dreams and visions, but I want to emphasize that God also uses them to communicate in our lives. Anyone can experience these, but one must ask God to teach them how to interpret what He is saying through them. Understanding your dreams can be challenging.

Now, in dreams and visions, God gave many in Biblical times and continues to provide them with today. Dreams are offered for different purposes, such as to restrain from evil (Genesis 20:3), reveal God's will (Genesis 28:11-22) to encourage (Judges 7:13-15), reveal the future (Genesis 37:5-10), or give instruction (Matthew 1:20).

Whether God speaks to you through His Word, Holy Spirit, or perhaps through a dream or vision, we must learn to understand and obey God's words! Neh'enah.

35

The Devil's Schemes!

"And I wrote this very thing to you, lest, when I came, I should have sorrow over those from whom I ought to have joy, having confidence in you all that my joy is the joy of you all. For out of much affliction and anguish of heart I wrote to you, with many tears, not that you should be grieved, but that you might know the love which I have so abundantly for you. But if anyone has caused grief, he has not grieved me, but all of you to some extent—not to be too severe. This punishment which was inflicted by the majority is sufficient for such a man, so that, on the contrary, you ought rather to forgive and comfort him, lest perhaps such a one be swallowed up with too much sorrow. Therefore I urge you to reaffirm your love to him. For to this end I also wrote, that I might put you to the test, whether you are obedient in all things. Now whom you forgive anything, I also forgive. For if indeed I have forgiven anything, I have forgiven that one for your sakes in the presence of Christ, lest Satan should take advantage of us; for we are not ignorant of his devices." (2 Corinthians 2:3-11)

In dealing with forgiving a brother who committed an incestuous sin against the Lord, the Apostle Paul, after rebuking such one, encourages the church to bring him now in and reaffirm him after his repentance.

The need to forgive such a person was now necessary, and Paul wanted to make sure that the church at Corinth was moving in forgiveness. If the church of Corinth would forgive the person, Paul would be more.

Paul's concern was that the church wouldn't have divisions, knowing that Satan could also take advantage of the situation. Plus, Paul notes, "...we are not ignorant of his devices."

Our Enemies!

When we study the Word of God as believers, we must always remember that we are called to please God in all things. I know that we are human-created beings, and I also know that, as Paul mentioned, there is no good thing in us. Perfection is not in us, but we strive to become like Jesus daily. We are called to hide ourselves in Christ in God!

Knowing this, we must be aware of the three enemies constantly trying to detour us from coming into the likeness of Jesus Christ, Our Lord. These enemies fight both inwardly and outwardly. Here they are: the world, the devil, and the flesh (our old nature.)

The goal of our enemy or enemies has been the same throughout history. He tries to seduce us into following a corrupt system of belief (the world), he tries to make us fear and believe his wicked ideas in our minds (the devil), and he is forever taking advantage of our weakness (of our flesh) and making us stumble continually.

In exposing the devil's schemes, one must realize that the devil is astute. He is not one to come out in plain sight and discover his tricks and methods of getting us away from our faith in Jesus.

For too long, many have believed that the devil tricks us with obvious things. He might, but I believe his tricks and schemes are a bit trickier than we think.

Allow me to outline some of these schemes the devil has been using for a pretty long time without the believer picking it up and discerning the way he has been causing the most significant damage in us who want to please Jesus.

Schemes!

1. The first scheme the devil loves to use is to fill our minds with doubt and fear. Nothing paralyzes a believer quicker and more efficiently than doubt and fear. With these two elements at work in our lives, God's plans will be hindered in us. Fear and doubt are fruits of the flesh; without faith, it is impossible to please God.

2. The enemy is a master in getting us to focus on instant gratification. Once again, the flesh, lacking self-control, will always fall into this trap. To have something right this minute, to have it now, has caused many to stumble severely. In relationships, in finances, in diets, etc. If we can't control ourselves, we will fall into instant gratification.

3. The enemy will also surround you with people who will negatively influence you. Some people seem to pull you away from Jesus. Their worldview on God, sin, culture, and religion doesn't come from a godly perspective. Their lives are choking the life out of yours!

4. The devil has an agenda, and in it, he wants to make sure you feel comfortable; his goal is that you live a life free of any commitments to Christ, his church, his will, and his ways. Only think of your needs, never mind what God desires for you.

5. The devil will also attempt to erode our confidence. He will continually beat you up on how many times you have failed, quit, or lacked what it takes to win. He is relentlessly self-deprecating your life until you finally give it all up!

6. The devil will also work on your habits, making you practice poor habits. For example, it keeps you up all night watching TV, using social media, and talking on the phone for hours on end so that you don't get up in the mornings to spend time with Jesus in prayer.

7. One of his most potent tactics must be this one: He will always keep your focus on the external things of life rather than on the internal ones. He will make your life so overwhelmed with what you don't have and what you want and make you forget what He has provided for you or desires for and from you.

8. Finally, he will take away the urgency from your life. He will make you believe that your life is going at a good pace the way it is. He will trap you into thinking that you are fine the way you are and that "God has a timing for everything!" So, you go on believing your manufactured fleshly thoughts while the world, your family, and even you are on your way to hell!

In closing, the Apostle Peter wrote, **"Be sober, be vigilant; because your adversary the devil walks about like a roaring lion, seeking whom he may devour."** (1 Peter 5:8)

The word of God calls all His servants to be sober and vigilant. While we are spiritually sleeping, someone is stealing our time, our money, our families, our futures, and our calling of God.

It is time to wake up to the devil's schemes and see if any of them are not taking us captive, and we don't even know it! Neh'enah.

36

Making Lasting, Life-Changing, God-Pleasing Changes!

"When His disciples heard it, they were greatly astonished, saying, "Who then can be saved?" But Jesus looked at them and said to them, "With men this is impossible, but with God all things are possible." (Matthew 19:25, 26)

Jesus said to him, "**If you can believe, all things are possible to him who believes.**" (Mark 9:23)

While meditating, I came across some exciting thoughts regarding miracles and overcoming impossibilities. I was intrigued by a few Scriptures and how they play a role in my life as an overcomer. Let's dive into this truth.

Who Can Be Saved?

The word "saved" means to be delivered from a present situation or threat. For example, our inner being. How can one be saved from our flesh? It is a fair question to ask. If one doesn't have a living relationship with God, they won't understand; and if they do have a relationship with God but have not been taught, they will also lack the knowledge of God to overcome.

So, for the one who lacks God's knowledge and wisdom, his life will be spent in an endless cycle of doing good works to appease the sinful nature that burns deep within; this man will still be trapped by selfishness and have no hope in the world. I can see this man throwing up his hands in the air and saying, "Following Jesus is impossible!" To this effect, Jesus said, "With men this is impossible, but with God all things are possible."

Flesh Can't Save Flesh!

Man is comprised of three elements: Spirit, Soul, and Body. God made human beings to be triune. He gave us a spirit, a soul, and a body. With the spirit, we connect with Him, with the soul (flesh) we express our feelings and emotions, and with the body we carry out the wishes of God or the flesh.

Now, the flesh, the carnal side to all of us, is unsanctified. This part can't be sanctified. It is made sinful from birth. This is the awful part of the human being known as the house of Satan, where God's Will is confronted.

Self (known as the flesh, soul, carnal nature, the old man) can't help you, and I overcome sin or its pleasures. There is no power to sustain you in the flesh. It is weak and it wars against all that is holy and divine!

When a sinful (lost) man or a woman is told to make changes to their life or else, though they may agree that they need to make changes in their lives, they lack the power to carry them out. Why? They lack the power to make changes because God is not present to enable the person. In their minds, they know they need to change, but in their hearts, they don't have the power to do so!

With Man, It Is Impossible!

Another thing to note is that no matter how famous, how much status or money, or how smart one may be, they don't have the capacity to change to a life that is pleasing to God. They can make social changes that society will accept, but concerning a relationship with God, it is impossible.

You have probably heard people saying, "I need to change my life and stop being this way!" Nevertheless, in their feeble attempt to upgrade their lives, they fail miserably. People think that by trying harder, they can get to the place they need to be. This can be very tiresome and overwhelming. So the point to all this is that a person can't make changes without God!

In sharing this powerful universal principle, Jesus said, **"If you can believe, all things are possible to him who believes."** This is a powerful, revelatory insight into God's mind.

If one can believe, but believe in what or in whom? Well, for starters, one must believe in Him and secondly, in His knowledge and wisdom. Whatever God tells you to do, say, or act in, this will be the process to a life that is pleasing to Him.

Transformation Begins Here!

"Humble yourselves in the sight of the Lord, and He will lift you up." (James 4:10)

Since flesh can't save flesh, the Spirit of God can release His power over you, if you so desire, and enable you to get the victory in any setting.

To humble oneself means to put God first. Whatever the situation, one must allow the Lord to be King and Lord; one must allow the Lord to drive our car (life), and we must confess and admit that we are terrible drivers (based on all the wrecks we have been in!).

Until we are clothed in true humility, we will not have a chance to make any lasting, God-pleasing changes.

It is true, flesh can't save flesh, but if we humble ourselves before God, He will take up our cause and enable us to do His will His way! Neh'enah.

37

Leadership for Our New Season!

"Then Joshua rose early in the morning; and they set out from Acacia Grove and came to the Jordan, he and all the children of Israel, and lodged there before they crossed over. So it was, after three days, that the officers went through the camp; and they commanded the people, saying, "When you see the ark of the covenant of the LORD your God, and the priests, the Levites, bearing it, then you shall set out from your place and go after it. Yet there shall be a space between you and it, about two thousand cubits by measure. Do not come near it, that you may know the way by which you must go, for you have not passed this way before." (Joshua 3:1-4)

Why Prayer Is an Important Key for the Upcoming Season.

For some, prayer is like a fresh cup of water; yet for others, it is foreign. When prayers to God are offered, they are usually short and with a request in mind. Some people don't like the art of personal praying. They don't like the idea that they are alone, calling upon God and waiting for some answer to come from somewhere from a God they don't even have a relationship with. If you don't know God personally, I can see why someone shuns praying alone.

For some reason, people have gotten the idea that prayer is a hotline to make requests for needs, etc. I'm not saying that prayer is not a channel to get a hold of God, but allow me to say that prayer is so much more than just a way to make requests to God. Prayer is more than just asking for God to fix your marriage, your business, or your life. Prayer is the believer's life-breath!

Prayer must become the means to an ever-growing and ever-increasing relationship with the King of Glory. Prayer is how one can know God's intentions, desires, and yearnings. To not understand this simple fact is to live the Christian life without guidance and spiritual leadership.

In Following God . . .

As we seek to know the Lord more intimately, we must be in much prayer and devotion.

Sitting in stillness before the Lord, waiting for His prophetic Word, or waiting for further instruction on a personal matter, etc., takes humility and patience. You must also know that spending quality time in the secret place of prayer will be rewarded.

Overcoming obstacles in prayer, such as a busy, worried, concerned, overwhelmed, biased, and selfish mind, is never easy. It will always present challenges to those who seek the Lord for guidance. Sitting still and waiting is already hard enough, but one must press through!

The Secret to a Focused-Prayer Mind

In the book of Matthew, it says: **"But you, when you pray, go into your room, and when you have shut your door, pray to your Father who is in the secret place; and your Father who sees in secret will reward you openly."** (Matthew 6:6)

The formula for a more effective way to pray is outlined here by the Master. When speaking to His true followers, Jesus advised, **"When you pray, go into your room, and when you have shut your door...".**

Shutting the door is needed as we focus on our heavenly Father. There is a very good reason for Jesus to teach us this. The Father appears as soon as we close the door (it may be a door in the mind, a worry perhaps).

Once we have Him before us, we can listen and receive fresh direction, revelation, or instructions.

Instructions for Our Tomorrows.

"Do not come near it, that you may know the way by which you must go, for you have not passed this way before."

Before Joshua crossed the Jordan River, the officers gave instructions. They didn't come as an enigma or a riddle; the word from the officers was very specific about what to do and how to proceed.

A fascinating observation is that the word came forth and advised the Hebrew children not to come near the ark of God, as it was leading them. The command continues, **"for you have not passed this way before."** Can you picture this event? The Lord was directing them through a new move of His Spirit. He was instructing them in this new venture, experience, or season. God will do this with you and me.

We may be clueless about what God is doing, but He will take the time to lead us through the unknown. He will open the map and guide us with His eye. We will not get lost if we follow His instructions.

I believe God still speaks this way and directs our steps this way. To pay attention to God's Word, to His Spirit, and His audible voice would be of significant gain for us. Knowing the strategy of God, the timing of God, and the purpose of God will enable us to be effective in our calling. Neh'enah.

38

Longing to See Who Jesus Is!

"Then Jesus entered and passed through Jericho. Now behold, there was a man named Zacchaeus who was a chief tax collector, and he was rich. And he sought to see who Jesus was, but could not because of the crowd, for he was of short stature. So he ran ahead and climbed up into a sycamore tree to see Him, for He was going to pass that way. And when Jesus came to the place, He looked up and saw him, and said to him, "Zacchaeus, make haste and come down, for today I must stay at your house." So he made haste and came down, and received Him joyfully." (Luke 19:1-6)

If there is something that the Holy Spirit impressed upon me this morning, it is this: Zacchaeus sought to see who Jesus was.

One thing is certain in seeking Jesus's person—we can't come to Him unless the Spirit of God invites us. I have experienced this in my walk with God. The inward longing to encounter God is totally a God thing!

This story repeatedly shows us that even sinners long to know who Jesus is. A sinner can be very stealthy in searching for God; however, the Lord knows everything. People can be fooled by sinners when they make their harsh rejection of Jesus. Sinners can pretend not to need anyone, for this would be normal behavior of anyone who wants to remain in control of their goods, their money, and their lives.

Remember what the Scripture says in John 6:44: "**No one can come to Me unless the Father who sent Me draws him; and I will raise him up on the last day.**" According to the words of Jesus, I do not doubt that the Father had moved the heart of Zacchaeus towards Christ.

Listen: You don't just wake up one day and out of the blue desire to see who Jesus is. This is a work of God.

The Hunger of the Spirit

If there is one thing about God's Spirit calling us unto something, it must be this: It is always accompanied by an insatiable fire of desire to touch the heart of God. I don't know how it all works, but I surely know when it is not on me.

The burning passion to seek Him at any cost will always overpower any other desire you might have. It will tear your agenda apart and make you change your meetings with people for the sake of meeting Christ. It will make you spend long hours in His presence, take elongated fasting times, and give you an appetite like you have never known for the Word of God. The hunger of the Spirit is what we need to advance His cause upon the earth.

Climbers!

"And he sought to see who Jesus was, but could not because of the crowd, for he was of short stature."

Desire is a powerful word that not many people know or understand. According to the Oxford Dictionary, desire means *"a strong feeling of wanting to have something or wishing for something to happen."*

The Scripture tells us that Zacchaeus, though rich, was still missing something in his life. I can only figure that the Father had drawn him to Christ as He passed through Jericho. No one could fill this void in this man's life; perhaps this day would be his day to find what his heart longed for.

Climbers are known for climbing and defying gravity. They are always at odds against the laws of nature and encounter obstacles to their achievement. This sounds like many of us.

This hungry man named Zaccheaus wanted to see Jesus, but had a few obstacles in front of him.

For starters, the crowds were blocking his view. He couldn't see Jesus from where he was standing. This was the first obstacle. Secondly, he was a man of short stature. This presented a problem in so many ways. He couldn't see because of the crowd and could have easily left and gone home without seeing Jesus, but he didn't. He was convinced that seeing Jesus was the most important thing to do at the time.

Accommodating the Move of God

Do you see what I am seeing?

Too many people don't have what it takes to see Jesus. They go so far that they turn back. You and I have done this. We start something fresh that God has birthed in us, and we don't follow through because of the opposition.

How often have we heard God tell us something prophetic, a Word or a promise, only to see it fall by the wayside? Why is this?

Much of what is aborted is due to our lack of brokenness. We lack a life of surrender, don't organize ourselves with the new instruction God has given us, and don't rearrange our lives to accommodate God's move in us. I have done it; you have done it!

Perseverance!

"So, he ran ahead and climbed up into a sycamore tree to see Him, for He was going to pass that way."

Since Zaccheaus was limited in stature, he climbed into a sycamore tree to see Jesus. How about that for creativity? This is a mark or characteristic of a man with vision and passion for Jesus.

When in desperation, one must learn to climb. Either we climb or miss God's move for our lives, ministries, and many other things God may bring our way.

Waiting Until You're Called by Name!

"And when Jesus came to the place, He looked up and saw him, and said to him, 'Zacchaeus, make haste and come down, for today I must stay at your house.'"

Desire is one thing; hunger to know God is another. Persevering to see God move is also very important, but nothing is more valuable than God saying your name, and for this, my friends, it takes time to wait before Him. After all the work has been done and the obstacles have been overcome, the arduous work of waiting upon God comes.

Many disqualified themselves from this, for they are too selfish and will not wait long before the Lord until He calls them out and gives them instruction. This holy moment will change your life forever. You will never be the same again. Neh'enah.

39

The Cost of Advancing!

"Then the children of Joseph spoke to Joshua, saying, 'Why have you given us only one lot and one share to inherit, since we are a great people, inasmuch as the LORD has blessed us until now?" So, Joshua answered them, "If you are a great people, then go up to the forest country and clear a place for yourself there in the land of the Perizzites and the giants, since the mountains of Ephraim are too confined for you." But the children of Joseph said, "The mountain country is not enough for us; and all the Canaanites who dwell in the land of the valley have chariots of iron, both those who are of Beth Shean and its towns and those who are of the Valley of Jezreel." And Joshua spoke to the house of Joseph, to Ephraim and Manasseh, saying, "You are a great people and have great power; you shall not have only one lot, but the mountain country shall be yours. Although it is wooded, you shall cut it down, and its farthest extent shall be yours; for you shall drive out the Canaanites, though they have iron chariots and are strong." (Joshua 17:14-18)

A Great People!

While meditating upon this portion of Scripture, I felt the Holy Spirit leading me into an inductive study of these events. As I pondered these insights, the Spirit of the Lord took me back to my early years of ministry. Allow me to share some thoughts on this.

In 1991, I was pastoring my first church; honestly, I was as green as they come. I didn't know very much about God's call, but I trusted God with my life in this endeavor. My heart was on fire for Jesus; all I wanted to do was please Him, and the cost didn't matter!

As the first two years rolled around, I sensed that perhaps I could find a better place (a more productive city) to set a church and make it grow. The place of my first pastorate was a small town. It was about 15 miles away from where I lived. Despite my thoughts of finding something better, I decided to keep doing the work.

I occasionally had this desperate moment when I felt I needed to move elsewhere. All this started to stem from a false sense of accomplishment, and I thought I needed to be rewarded for my good deeds. Yet no one took notice. I started to gain some confidence and felt that I deserved more than I had attained. The feeling of abandonment started to affect my heart, and I began to see my task (ministry) with a different attitude (not a good one).

What was happening to me?

What was happening to me was that I was growing within, but I needed to express that growth outwardly. I needed to take some crucial steps of faith to align my hands with my heart.

This learning experience began many growing challenges in my spiritual and ministry life.

Growing!

"Then the children of Joseph spoke to Joshua, saying, 'Why have you given us only one lot and one share to inherit, since we are a great people, inasmuch as the LORD has blessed us until now?"

While the people of God continued to move forward into their promised land, mainly the children of Joseph, they began feeling the need to expand into more territory, thus the complaint against Joshua saying, "**Why have you give us only one lot and one share to inherit, since we are a great people...**"

When I read this, I saw myself in it. The sense that you are now superior to others and need special attention to accommodate what God is doing with you has always been something to reckon with.

"So, Joshua answered them, 'If you are a great people, then go up to the forest country and clear a place for yourself there in the land of the Perizzites and the giants, since the mountains of Ephraim are too confined for you."

Alignment with God!

Joshua essentially said, "If you say that you are that great, then go and clear a place for yourself in the land of the Perizzites and the giants, being that you say where you presently are is too confined for you!"

The word confined means *to press or be pressed.*

These emotions often have a way of presenting change in our lives. Sometimes, it is just us; sometimes, it is just the circumstances; and sometimes, it is God moving in us to get us to where He needs us to be.

Sometimes, during these experiences, our hearts can cry; something must change! Other times, we silence it by saying, This is how life will be for me! Maybe others can enlarge, but not me!

What Is Really Happening?

What is happening is that God has opened your heart to fresh revelation of Himself and placed desires in your heart that were never there. Just like anything God does, it starts in the spirit of man, and through faith, brokenness, and obedience, one enters their promised territory!

Deep desires and longings for something can be caused by the Lord provoking you to take the necessary steps.

One must know that God is moving them into greater things, but must meet God at the place of faith, brokenness, and obedience.

The Challenge to Make a Change!

But the children of Joseph said, "The mountain country is not enough for us; and all the Canaanites who dwell in the land of the valley have chariots of iron, both those who are of Beth Shean and its towns and those who are of the Valley of Jezreel."

The minute one expresses what God wants to do, the challenge to make the necessary changes follows. Many will be challenged to pay a certain price to advance. If God places in your heart to take a mission trip to another country, one must deal with the cost first. What will it take for me to get there? How much will it cost me financially, emotionally, physically, spiritually, etc.?

In the case of the tribe of Joseph, they immediately said, **"The country is not enough for us, and the Canaanites have chariots of iron."** It is impressive to see how our attitudes are altered when the time to act comes. Many excuses are given, probably because of fear, doubt, or unbelief.

Getting Serious With God's Vision!

There always seems to be a time when we play games with the Lord, but the time will come when He speaks to us and directs us bolder, more affirmatively.

"And Joshua spoke to the house of Joseph, to Ephraim and Manasseh, saying, "You are a great people and have great power; you shall not have only one lot, but the mountain country shall be yours. Although it is wooded, you shall cut it down, and its farthest extent shall be yours; for you shall drive out the Canaanites, though they have iron chariots and are strong."

If you notice, Joshua got bolder and said, "You are a great people and have great power. You will not only have one lot, but the mountain country shall be yours." Sometimes, we need to hear God's voice express what He sees us doing. Sometimes, a leader needs to shake and challenge us to greater heights. The tribe of Joseph couldn't see the possibilities or the potential.

Then Joshua closes his conversation with this: "Although it is wooded, you shall cut it down, and its farthest extent shall be yours; for you shall drive out the Canaanites, though they have iron chariots and are strong."

To the Degree that Wood Is Cut, Is to the Degree We Gain Dominion!

Hearing the (prophetic) Word is the first step to move in God's revelation. Once we hear God's instruction by His Spirit, we follow His leadership. The Word comes into our inner man (spirit-man) and then we are to believe (Have the faith of God) in what we are being asked to do or how to act. Thirdly, we surrender to what we are being told to do (this is called brokenness). Without brokenness, God's purpose will not flow from us. Finally, we must walk in obedience despite the impossibilities.

This is how advancement happens for all who love the Lord. We are called to advance His glory upon the earth. It is not easy, but it is not impossible either. We must do His will His way! Unless we embrace His ways, nothing will make it happen. Neh'enah.

40

Cultural Christianity!

"And He went through the cities and villages, teaching, and journeying toward Jerusalem. Then one said to Him, "Lord, are there few who are saved?" And He said to them, "Strive to enter through the narrow gate, for many, I say to you, will seek to enter and will not be able. When once the Master of the house has risen up and shut the door, and you begin to stand outside and knock at the door, saying, 'Lord, Lord, open for us,' and He will answer and say to you, 'I do not know you, where you are from,' then you will begin to say, 'We ate and drank in Your presence, and You taught in our streets.' But He will say, 'I tell you I do not know you, where you are from. Depart from Me, all you workers of iniquity.'" (Luke 13:23-27)

The other day, cultural Christianity was mentioned while having dinner with a friend.

This is an interesting set of words; depending on which side of the fence you stand on, it could have a negative or positive connotation.

Cultural Christianity, to my understanding, is a type of pseudo-Christianity. It is a good way to convince oneself that one is a good person because one puts on the Christian label and appreciates all that comes with the package, such as good biblical practices, morality, and responsibility in daily life.

Many believe that attending a Christian church rather than any other religious institution is good and makes them better people. I have sat in meetings with professional people who, once they find out I'm a minister, say, I go to church, too. Of course, they say this after making mention of their party lifestyle, drinking binges, womanizing, and foul language.

These so-called Christians (by label only) are not following Jesus; they are following their flesh, their carnal desires; they will only give until it starts to cost them something! These people make up most of the people in your local churches today. They make up 97% of those sitting in congregations today. If you say, Pastor David, you are exaggerating! Trust me, if I am, it is not by much.

I find in the Scriptures that the same spirit of carnality we face today was alive and well in the days of Jesus. Allow me to share some insight into this.

Are There Few Who Are Saved?

"And He went through the cities and villages, teaching, and journeying toward Jerusalem. Then one said to Him, "Lord, are there few who are saved?"

Here's an interesting scene: Jesus speaks in different villages and teaches about the kingdom when someone suddenly asks, Lord, are there few who are saved? Now, why would anyone ask this question regarding salvation? Why would someone ask about the number of those entering the kingdom? I am unsure why this was asked, but it is sufficient to say that Jesus replied.

In his response, Jesus didn't give a set number of how many would be saved, but did instruct and say, "Strive to enter through the narrow gate, for many, I say to you, will seek to enter and will not be able. When once the Master of the house has risen up and shut the door, and you begin to stand outside and knock at the door, saying, 'Lord, Lord, open for us,' and He will answer and say to you, 'I do not know you, where you are from...'"

Regarding **"the entering in,"** Jesus makes it a point to say that one must strive to enter through a narrow gate. He adds, **"Many will seek to enter and will not be able to."** What does this mean? No one can come to God unless invited, but once asked, they will have the grace to step into this walk. If they accept the decision and follow through by faith, they will be able to enter in. They will miss out if they decide it is too narrow to walk through, meaning they are not willing to pay the price to step into it. Later in life, they will say to themselves, I want to do it now, but they won't be able to. One can only come to God when they are invited!

Once the Master Has Risen Up!

Once judgment comes and everyone stands before God to give account, those who turned down the invitation will be standing outside knocking at the door saying, **"Lord, Lord, open for us!"** He will answer and say, **"I do not know you, where you are from..."**

Please think about this. A whole group of people knew about Jesus, heard about the kingdom of God, and learned about a narrow gate, yet they didn't want any of it. They loved themselves more!

Is it any wonder that the Master of the house, once he shut the door and then those late comers started knocking, said to them, **"I do not know you, where you are from?"** Can you imagine 97% of our so-called Christians, or cultural Christians, hearing God say to them, I Do Not Know You!

Playing Religious Games!

Many believers have mastered what I call religious games. Today, people attend church for a good old time of social interactions, not to meet Jesus! These churches are filled with people looking for wives, husbands, business leads, opportunities to advance their business or social causes. The modern church of today has become a cesspool for selfish gain! What a mock!

Well, the day of reckoning had finally arrived for all religious game players in the times of Jesus... look at this: **He will answer and say to you, 'I do not know you, where you are from,' then you will begin to say, 'We ate and drank in Your presence, and You taught in our streets.' But He will say, 'I tell you I do not know you, where you are from. Depart from Me, all you workers of iniquity.'"**

After Jesus responded to those knocking at the door and pleading their case before the Master of the house, saying, "We ate and drank in Your presence, and You taught in our streets," Jesus still said the same thing to them: "I do not know you, where you are from."

You see, in these religious games, it is possible to be part of a church fellowship, participate in Bible classes, and serve. These religious game players pressed in and said, "You taught in our streets!" In other words, we were there for you, Jesus. We participated; we sat under your teaching—what do you mean you don't know us?

Unless the life of Jesus is in your spirit-man, unless you are walking and living in resurrection power, you have no part in Jesus, and it doesn't matter what church you belong to.

Depart from Me!

"But He will say, 'I tell you I do not know you, where you are from. Depart from Me, all you workers of iniquity.'"

There will come a time when all these 97% will face their carnality. They will be judged accordingly. They can fool people and even the pastor; however, the day will come when they see the foolishness of their own hearts! Neh'enah.

41

From God's Perspective! – Part 1

"If ye then be risen with Christ, seek those things which are above, where Christ sitteth on the right hand of God. Set your affection on things above, not on things on the earth. For ye are dead, and your life is hid with Christ in God. When Christ, who is our life, shall appear, then shall ye also appear with him in glory." (Colossians 3:1-4 KJV)

"If you then have been raised with Christ [to a new life, thus sharing His resurrection from the dead], **aim at and seek the** [rich, eternal treasures] **that are above, where Christ is, seated at the right hand of God.** [Ps. 110:1.] **And set your minds and keep them set on what is above (the higher things), not on the things that are on the earth. For** [as far as this world is concerned] **you have died, and your** [new, real] **life is hidden with Christ in God. When Christ, Who is our life, appears, then you also will appear with Him in** [the splendor of His] **glory."** (Colossians 3:1-4 Amplified Version)

In pondering the condition of the church today, I've been praying and crying out for a genuine revival in the hearts of His people, for a deeper life in God, a more profound knowledge of Jesus as a Person, and His desires for us who believe.

Unless the Lord puts the desire in your heart to seek Him, you can't pursue Him. One can try to become more spiritual in their Christian walk, for one, because we are challenged or made to feel guilty about our walk with Christ. I still believe that unless God, by His Spirit, draws us to Christ, we can't follow Him. It is impossible!

Most of the so-called believers today are not even saved. There are probably about 97% of Christians today who claim to know Christ but have never been born again. Due to this pseudo form of Christianity, these so-called believers find it difficult to keep up with the demands of God. It is easier to get mad at the leadership of a church than to deal with the reality of their condition.

Christianity: Does it Work or Not?

I know this question should not even be asked this late in the game, but I have discovered that much of what we see today in the world, as far as Christianity is concerned, is that for so many professed Christians, this religion is not working for them.

People have bought into the idea that God will fix their lives, marriages, careers, businesses, or ministries. When this doesn't happen, they complain, criticize, and finally fall away from the faith they professed. This is seen worldwide because people have been taught a different Jesus.

Too often, people see life from their perspective: what they want, desire, intend to do, etc. This is a recipe for disappointment. The error stems from our wants; we tell God what we want and expect Him to fulfill those wants. This will never work, or at least, not for a long time.

Seeing Life from God's Perspective

In Colossians 3:1-4, let us learn together about the importance of seeing life from God's perspective.

"If ye then be risen with Christ..." – Herein lies the foundation for true life. Without this one experience, the Bible doesn't mean anything to you. Our life has no existence, meaning, or purpose without being raised with Christ. You may have a natural life, but no spiritual life. Remember the words of Jesus, God is Spirit, and those who worship Him must worship in spirit and truth. (John 4:24). Everything that God will ever do in you has to do with this first principle of being awakened or resurrected by the life of God, which is now within you.

"...Seek those things which are above, where Christ sitteth on the right hand of God." Providing that you have been born again by the Spirit of the Lord, the counsel is to seek those things which are above. What things is Paul referring to? These are the things that pertain to His kingdom, not your kingdom. These are things that pertain to life and godliness. Things that have to do with your life in Him. Some of the things would be: His will, His desires, His emotions, His plan, and His strategy.

What will you do next once you discover all that God has outlined for your life, specifically, for a particular season?

"Set your affection on things above, not on things on the earth." The original version says that once you find what you should be and do, you must set your affections on them. What does it mean to set, and what are affections? The word set means concentrating, while the word affections means your mind.

Paul further reveals in the Book of Romans: "For those who live according to the flesh set their minds on the things of the flesh, but those who live according to the Spirit, the things of the Spirit. For to be carnally minded is death, but to be spiritually minded is life and peace. Because the carnal mind is enmity against God; for it is not subject to the law of God, nor indeed can be. So then, those who are in the flesh cannot please God." (Romans 8:5-8)

The things of the earth speak of the list of things you want, the things you prefer, things that you desire and are seeking for your interest and gain.

"For ye are dead, and your life is hid with Christ in God." One of the most significant challenges for any faithful servant of God is following Jesus to places that are inconvenient to our flesh. We must never forget that Christ is always first in all things, our job is to follow Him wherever He goes.

As we pursue His heart, remember that we are hidden in Christ. He is the visible One; we are hidden. It is the same for all we do in His Name (His works) and our spiritual battles. When the devil comes knocking at your door, send Jesus to open the door. Not even the devil can find you when you are hidden in Christ! Neh'enah.

42

From God's Perspective! – Part 2

"In the beginning was the Word, and the Word was with God, and the Word was God. He was in the beginning with God. All things were made through Him, and without Him nothing was made that was made. In Him was life, and the life was the light of men." (John 1:1-4)

"And He said to them, "You are from beneath; I am from above. You are of this world; I am not of this world." (John 8:23)

Jesus was not from this world. But those who heard Him didn't know that. He understood all things. He knew the beginning from the end. When He spoke, He always spoke as Someone with authority. We now know why and will begin to understand God's way of thinking more clearly.

You see, to enter into God's life and walk in it with purpose and victory, one must see it from God's point of view. We must see life as God sees it. If we fail to do this, we will always wonder why our lives have turned out the way they have and not live in the full plan God had destined for us as believers.

Jesus taught us how to think, how to see, how to speak, and how to act in our walk. He covered all the bases. Let us look at this:

"Look at the birds of the air, for they neither sow nor reap nor gather into barns; yet your heavenly Father feeds them. Are you not of more value than they? Which of you by worrying can add one cubit to his stature?
"So why do you worry about clothing? Consider the lilies of the field, how they grow: they neither toil nor spin; and yet I say to you that even

Solomon in all his glory was not arrayed like one of these. Now if God so clothes the grass of the field, which today is, and tomorrow is thrown into the oven, will He not much more clothe you, O you of little faith? "Therefore do not worry, saying, 'What shall we eat?' or 'What shall we drink?' or 'What shall we wear?' For after all these things the Gentiles seek. For your heavenly Father knows that you need all these things. But seek first the kingdom of God and His righteousness, and all these things shall be added to you." (Matthew 6:26-33)

What Is Truly Important?

One of the main things I noticed was how Jesus spoke about the kingdom of God and its values. When He spoke, Jesus never seemed riled up or worried about this natural life. He spoke as someone who was in control of everything around Him.

Why would or could anyone speak in such a manner? How can one be so tranquil regarding life's most important matters – or were they that important?

Things are important to someone when their hearts are set on them. If one's faculties, heart, and mind are set on earthly things, then I can understand why someone would be worried or overly concerned about such matters. Now, if the person has no regard for lesser earthly things, he would be free to soar in another realm.

Our Lord Jesus Christ, the Father's Only Begotten Son, understood the structure of all things. He knew where everything originated and how everything would end. This knowledge puts anyone in a better place physically, emotionally, spiritually, and economically.

I believe that when we enter the life of God, a drop of His mercy upon us will give us the understanding of His intentions for creation. The Lord Jesus held everything in the palm of His hand. Listen to this: **"He is the** image of the invisible God, the firstborn over all creation. For by Him all things were created that are in heaven and that are on earth, visible and invisible, whether thrones or dominions or principalities or powers. All things were created through Him and for Him. And He is before all things, and in Him all things consist. And He is the head of the body, the church, who is the beginning, the firstborn from the dead, that in all things He may have the preeminence. For it pleased the Father that in Him all the fullness should dwell, and by Him to reconcile all things to Himself, by Him, whether things on earth or things in heaven, having made peace through the blood of His cross." (Colossians 1:15-20)

The fact that Jesus knew the beginning from the end placed Him over humanity's obstacles and challenges. He was not caught up with the lesser things of life but with the things that the Father considered of the most significant value.

Victory Rests In Our Knowledge of Christ

Regarding our text above, Jesus said, "**Look at the birds of the air, for they neither sow nor reap nor gather into barns; yet your heavenly Father feeds them. Are you not of more value than they? Which of you, by worrying, can add one cubit to his stature?**"

Jesus knew that humanity seeks outer things. Whether it be food, shelter, or clothing, humanity has an instinct to seek these things. Man can't help but be selfish. Is it any wonder why there is continual worrying and fighting for more of the outer than that which feeds the spirit of man? It is natural for man to worry when there is a lack, unless he has caught a glimpse of something greater.

Notice this: Jesus turns the hearer's attention to the birds of the air. He further explains how they neither sow nor reap nor gather into barns; yet the heavenly Father feeds them! He adds, "**Are you not of more value than they?**" This is something to ponder.

Whether one cares to look at birds as a comparison or not, Jesus essentially says, **"Look, anything God creates He feeds and takes care of."** To feed means to nourish, to make to grow. If He cares for birds whom He values, how much more valuable is humanity?

Once we realize our value before God, which can only come through the revelation of the Spirit of God into our spirit, we will begin to soar to greater heights, not to mention worrying less about outer things!

Worrying Can Be Overcome By Knowing Our Value

Whatever we set our hearts on, this will always be the fountain that dictates our mindset. We can only think as far as our hearts can capture. We can't pass our heart's vision or longing. **"For as he thinketh in his heart, so is he."** (Proverbs 23:7)

When it comes to worrying about a matter, a thing, or even our future, in whatever state our heart is in, this will be our fountain of truth. If Jesus is God, then trust Him. If your heart is set on external earthly things, this will be your god, thus the worrying. Neh'enah.

43

When God Tests the Promise!

Now behold, two of them were traveling that same day to a village called Emmaus, which was seven miles from Jerusalem. And they talked together of all these things which had happened. So it was, while they conversed and reasoned, that Jesus Himself drew near and went with them. But their eyes were restrained, so that they did not know Him. And He said to them, "What kind of conversation is this that you have with one another as you walk and are sad?" (Luke 24:13-17)

My brethren, count it all joy when you fall into various trials, knowing that the testing of your faith produces patience. But let patience have its perfect work, that you may be perfect and complete, lacking nothing." (James 1:2-4)

"In this, you greatly rejoice, though now for a little while, if need be, you have been grieved by various trials, that the genuineness of your faith, being much more precious than gold that perishes, though it is tested by fire, may be found to praise, honor, and glory at the revelation of Jesus Christ..." (1 Peter 1:6, 7)

During the last few days of prayer and study, the Holy Spirit has caused my spirit to capture this picture of what the **"testing of our faith"** is like. In meditation in His Word, I saw the story above, of these two disciples walking back home to Emmaus.

These servants of Jesus who heard and, followed the teachings of Jesus, came to a sudden reality when Christ (who had made many promises while alive) had now been crucified and their expectations and dreams shattered to pieces. Everything promised was now just an illusion and now they found themselves back to where they started – with nothing!

Natural vs. Spiritual

There is such a thing as hearing with the natural ear and responding, and yes, there is also a thing as hearing in the spirit (with the ears of the spirit) and responding. One form of listening (natural) is for this life; another form of listening (spiritual) is for the spirit man and is eternal. Don't get these two things mixed up!

To hear Jesus in real time, would be to say, that Jesus said that we would reign with Him. He also said, Where I am, you will be there also. One can hear that and think, "It's happening today or tomorrow!" But spiritual people would see beyond that and say, "The promise is on its way!" Mind you, it takes the faith of God to be patient and wait for the promise.

Your Faith Will Be Tested!

These two disciples on the road to Emmaus were literally broken and fell into a deep sadness over the matter that Jesus had died; their faith was being tested. The Scripture says, **"And they talked together of all these things which had happened. "**

When you truly are engaged with the Spirit of God and the Lord Jesus is leading you, your life becomes just like these two disciples – you will also be tested by every word you heard and every promise that was made to you by the Lord; it will all be tested.

Please don't think that Jesus promises you something and that you won't be tested because of it. He will test your faith and develop it so that you may learn to walk with full assurance that Christ is.

Forced to Trust When All Has Gone Wrong!

"My brethren, count it all joy when you fall into various trials, knowing that the testing of your faith produces patience. But let patience have its perfect work, that you may be perfect and complete, lacking nothing." (James 1:2-4)

As you look at your disappointments, your shattered dreams, your plans destroyed, and your life still facing opposition, know that God is producing patience in you and making you perfect and complete, so that you don't lack anything.

When we get tired of holding on to the hem of His garment, then, that's when we truly must begin to hold on to it!

Jesus Drops In!

As the two servants kept walking and talking about all the things that happened back in Jerusalem, Jesus came in on the conversation, but they didn't know Him. "So it was, while they conversed and reasoned, that Jesus Himself drew near and went with them. But their eyes were restrained, so that they did not know Him. And He said to them, "What kind of conversation is this that you have with one another as you walk and are sad?"

Jesus knew exactly who these servants were, what they were feeling now, and the condition of their hearts. Jesus knew that they were sad! The word sad means to look gloomy.

You see, the Lord knows about all the promises He made; He knows exactly how we received them – whether in the flesh or the spirit. This makes the difference as we learn to walk by faith with God.

Let me add that most of our disillusions and broken or shattered expectations, come our way because we do not appropriate what God said by faith. [see Hebrews 4:2]

What Things?

"Then the one whose name was Cleopas answered and said to Him, "Are You the only stranger in Jerusalem, and have You not known the things which happened there in these days?"
And He said to them, "What things?"
So they said to Him, "The things concerning Jesus of Nazareth, who was a Prophet mighty in deed and word before God and all the people, and how the chief priests and our rulers delivered Him to be condemned to death and crucified Him. But we were hoping that it was He who was going to redeem Israel. Indeed, besides all this, today is the third day since these things happened. Yes, and certain women of our company, who arrived at the tomb early, astonished us. When they did not find His body, they came saying that they had also seen a vision of angels who said He was alive. And certain of those who were with us went to the tomb and found it just as the women had said; but Him they did not see." (Luke 24:18-24)

These disciples were so sad and disappointed that they were beyond repair as one would say. Yet, God can make anyone stand!

These two disciples had been following the life of Jesus closely. They were convinced that Jesus would redeem Israel. Listen: **"But we were hoping that it was He who was going to redeem Israel."**

Hoping is an act of the flesh; it is not spirit. Many of us set our affections on earthly things and when they break down or don't come to pass, we are devasted. That is what a person gets when they put their hope on earthly things!

Hope doesn't believe in the supernatural acts of God; it only depends on what can be seen. Isn't it any wonder that they said to Jesus, **"And certain of those who were with us went to the tomb and found it just as the women had said; but Him they did not see?"**

When the Spirit Reminds Us of His Great Works!

Then He said to them, "O foolish ones, and slow of heart to believe in all that the prophets have spoken! Ought not the Christ to have suffered these things and to enter into His glory?" And beginning at Moses and all the Prophets, He expounded to them in all the Scriptures the things concerning Himself." (Luke 24:25-27)

After hearing the complaining, whining, and unbelief in action, Jesus proceeded to educate these two disciples on the matters of faith.

For starters, He begins by reminding them of what the prophets said concerning Christ.

He further pressed in to dismantle their sadness; He continued teaching them of all the powerful stuff God did in Moses' day and all the things the prophets of old did. He expounded to them about Himself and how now He had risen but they couldn't see it for they were blinded by the false hope of their dreams!

For a Little While . . .

"In this, you greatly rejoice, though now for a little while, if need be, you have been grieved by various trials, that the genuineness of your faith, being much more precious than gold that perishes, though it is tested by fire, may be found to praise, honor, and glory at the revelation of Jesus Christ..." (1 Peter 1:6, 7)

Always keep in mind that most trials are only for a little while. Not sure exactly what that means, but I know that God will press us up to where we learn the lesson He wants us to learn. If we stay humble and teachable, it may be that the trial is shortened.

These disciple's faith was being tested "**for a little while.**" Jesus had to come in and teach them about all that God had promised. He had to remind them that all these things needed to take place so that their destinies could be completed as they followed Him.

As I close, keep in mind that God is after developing a genuine faith in us. This is of more value to Him than anything else we might set our hearts on. Neh'enah.

44

Why Has the Lord Defeated Us Today? - Part 1

"Now Israel went out to battle against the Philistines and encamped beside Ebenezer; and the Philistines encamped in Aphek. Then the Philistines put themselves in battle array against Israel. And when they joined battle, Israel was defeated by the Philistines, who killed about four thousand men of the army in the field. And when the people had come into the camp, the elders of Israel said, "Why has the LORD defeated us today before the Philistines? Let us bring the ark of the covenant of the LORD from Shiloh to us, that when it comes among us it may save us from the hand of our enemies." So the people sent to Shiloh, that they might bring from there the ark of the covenant of the LORD of hosts, who dwells between the cherubim. And the two sons of Eli, Hophni and Phinehas, were there with the ark of the covenant of God." (1 Samuel 4:1-4)

During my quiet time this morning, I read a passage of Scripture that I found somewhat troubling and puzzling.

The Bible says that Israel faced off against the Philistines; everyone took their positions and prepared for a big fight. When the battle started, the Philistines pulled off a shocker; they defeated Israel decisively. Israel never saw it coming, let alone lose the battle, and four thousand men were killed as well.

As they headed back to the camp, the first thing they asked was, Why has the Lord defeated us today before the Philistines?

I want you to give your full attention to these words spoken by the captain; within them, you'll find the key to every victory. Please notice how the leader was quick to say, "Why has the Lord defeated us..." Do you see this?

When God Is Against You!

One sign of the times I've noticed is how believers today are so disconnected from the responsibility given to them by God to walk with Him. Many believers still think that once salvation happens, their lives continue on autopilot; yes, they believe that since Jesus already paid the price for our sins, all we must do is enjoy the ride until we get to heaven! My friends, this is a very popular message in the modern church today! As good as this message sounds, it's one of the devil's biggest lies, and believers are buying it in truckloads!

Why would God be against His people? Isn't this a great question? Would you ask yourself the same thing? If things weren't going right in your life, wouldn't you wonder the following: If God saved me and bought me with such a great price, then I belong to Him. Nothing by any means can touch me now, unless God, my Owner, gives permission to anyone or anything to come my way and hurt me. This is how our theology should flow.

Clearly, many have faltered in this and quickly turn away from God's protection, beginning to be led by false teachers spreading false demonic-inspired teachings and man-made reasonings, which, in my opinion, are inspired by Satan himself, all with the goal of confusing God's saints and leading them down a path of bondage once again!

Listen to the Elders!

"The elders of Israel said, "Why has the LORD defeated us today before the Philistines?" (1 Samuel 4:3)

Apparently, the Lord was displeased with Eli and his sons, Hophni and

Phinehas. A judgment had been declared, and God had withdrawn His hand from Israel. Listen to this judgment given to little Samuel by the Lord while serving at the temple under the Priest Eli: "Then the LORD said to Samuel: "Behold, I will do something in Israel at which both ears of everyone who hears it will tingle. In that day I will perform against Eli all that I have spoken concerning his house, from beginning to end. For I have told him that I will judge his house forever for the iniquity which he knows, because his sons made themselves vile, and he did not restrain them. And therefore, I have sworn to the house of Eli that the iniquity of Eli's house shall not be atoned for by sacrifice or offering forever." (1 Samuel 3:11-14)

When the elders of Israel inquired and asked, "**Why has the Lord defeated us today before the Philistines?**" they didn't say, "Why has the devil or demons or witches, or hexes, or spells, defeated us? No! They said, "Why has the Lord... defeated us?"

Judged!

I wholeheartedly believe that most of the defeats you and I will face are nothing more than signs of our falling away from God's divine order; a judgment being applied to us for our disobedience.

Most of our struggles usually result from our disobedience. God has spoken to us about a certain matter, and we ignore His Spirit; in response, judgment often follows.

The elders sensed that something was not aligned with God's revealed will. They realized a change had taken place. God's favor was no longer helping them but working against them.

As I conclude this first meditation on this subject, will you ask yourself, Is God working with me or against me?

Before passing judgment on anyone or anything, or before blame starts, it's wise to ask ourselves: Have I disobeyed God willingly, and could I now be judged for it? If you have rebelled against God's divine order, repent of it, and be restored! Neh'enah.

45

Why Has the Lord Defeated Us Today? - Part 2

"...the elders of Israel said, "Why has the LORD defeated us today before the Philistines? Let us bring the ark of the covenant of the LORD from Shiloh to us, that when it comes among us it may save us from the hand of our enemies." So the people sent to Shiloh, that they might bring from there the ark of the covenant of the LORD of hosts, who dwells between the cherubim. And the two sons of Eli, Hophni and Phinehas, were there with the ark of the covenant of God." (1 Samuel 4:3, 4)

As we have been covering this sad story of defeat to the Israelites, one can only question and ask, "**If God is our God and we are His people, wouldn't He defend us from our enemies? I mean, if we are the apple of His eye, why would He allow us to be defeated in such a manner?**"

This would be a legit line of questioning; we would not be out of line if we were to pray that way. However, God would be quick to point out the why, the underlying reason why this happened in such a manner. The real question now would be: Are we ready to hear the truth?

Setting Our Eyes on Props!

"Let us bring the ark of the covenant of the LORD from Shiloh to us, that when it comes among us it may save us from the hand of our enemies."

In my years of ministering the Word of God as a leader, pastor, or itinerant teacher, I have seen people fixate on a particular person, church, group, or specific type of service (such as healing or deliverance services). People often chase after things or people, but rarely pursue Jesus, the Lord

Himself. They believe that attending a specific meeting or speaking with a particular individual will solve their problems, and so on.

These believers are looking for props rather than Jesus. What is a prop? A prop is a pole or beam used for support or to hold something in place, usually not a vital part of what it sustains. A prop is anything other than Jesus!

When the Philistines defeated the Israelites and left them in a state of confusion, dazed and bewildered, they said, **"Let us bring the ark of the covenant of the Lord!"** Remember that the Ark of the Covenant represented the very presence of God. In other words, they were essentially saying, Let us bring the big guns, let us bring the Shekinah glory of God, and let us put these Philistines out of their misery once and for all!

When Does the Presence of God Become a Prop?

The presence of God was represented by the Ark of the Covenant, which the priest moved around by carrying it in processions. Whether it was for worship or battle, the Ark of the Covenant would go before them.

To answer the question I mentioned earlier, the Ark of the Covenant is just a prop when it contains nothing. Outwardly, the Ark was there, but its true power was gone! God was no longer with Israel. The Ark of the Covenant had become nothing more than a prop!

I believe many believers today are doing exactly that; they are captivated by props! They have their favorite pastor, church, service, worship songs, and so on. God's presence isn't there, but they keep relying on these props to get through tough times.

Instead of questioning, evaluating, and spending time in God's presence for answers, they run to their props. They fall prostrate before them, thinking that their answers will come from such props!

Props Are Displays of Our Flesh!

"And when the ark of the covenant of the LORD came into the camp, all Israel shouted so loudly that the earth shook." (1 Samuel 4:5)

As the Ark of the Covenant arrived from Shiloh, all Israel went bananas; the Scripture says that they shouted so loud that the earth shook! They were so excited to have this Ark present that they thought for sure the battle would now be won against the Philistines.

Listen, my friends, the Ark of the Covenant was simply a wooden box covered in gold. There was nothing special about it, except that God said He would use it to symbolize His presence among His people. Now, if the Lord said, "I'm not showing up," then all it would be is a plain wooden box. You cannot put your trust in anything created, only in the Creator Jesus!

If we put our trust in anything other than Jesus, we will be gravely and painfully disappointed. Israel was about to discover this.

Get Alone with God!

Whenever a believer mentions that life is difficult or that they're facing challenges in their walk of faith, they often quickly seek prayer and counsel from man. I'm not against asking for guidance and prayer, if this servant of God has spent some quality time with Jesus in private first before consulting any man or woman.

In closing, be careful with fleshly counsel lest you find yourself resting on some prop! Neh'enah.

46

Why Has the Lord Defeated Us Today? - Part 3

"Now when the Philistines heard the noise of the shout, they said, "What does the sound of this great shout in the camp of the Hebrews mean?" Then they understood that the ark of the LORD had come into the camp. So the Philistines were afraid, for they said, "God has come into the camp!" And they said, "Woe to us! For such a thing has never happened before. Woe to us! Who will deliver us from the hand of these mighty gods? These are the gods who struck the Egyptians with all the plagues in the wilderness. Be strong and conduct yourselves like men, you Philistines, that you do not become servants of the Hebrews, as they have been to you. Conduct yourselves like men, and fight!"
So the Philistines fought, and Israel was defeated, and every man fled to his tent. There was a very great slaughter, and there fell of Israel thirty thousand foot soldiers. Also the ark of God was captured; and the two sons of Eli, Hophni and Phinehas, died." (1 Samuel 4:6-11)

What was the result of all the shouting when the Ark of the Covenant was brought into the battle from Shiloh? What was the point? If we can't be honest with ourselves and with God, then we don't stand a chance against the enemy.

It's like many church services today—people create the perfect atmosphere, have the right song list, deliver motivational messages, and shout along to worship songs, yet where is the victory? Most of what people call victory is just a fleeting display of fleshly motivation without the Spirit of revelation.

How do I know that?

I have been in services where all the aspects mentioned above are happening. People sway back and forth to the beat of the music, agree with everything the preacher says, but sadly, there are no tears in those believers' eyes. There is no repentance, no brokenness, no conviction of sin and compromise. No fire in the room that is sending laborers into the harvest. It's truly a sad sight to behold!

Shouting Will Cover Up Only for a While!

"Now when the Philistines heard the noise of the shout, they said, "What does the sound of this great shout in the camp of the Hebrews mean?" Then they understood that the ark of the LORD had come into the camp. So the Philistines were afraid, for they said, "God has come into the camp!" And they said, "Woe to us! For such a thing has never happened before. Woe to us! Who will deliver us from the hand of these mighty gods? These are the gods who struck the Egyptians with all the plagues in the wilderness."

Have you ever met people who are always struggling and constantly asking for prayer? It's like it almost always happens to them every week. They are frequently up and down in their spiritual walk and can't find victory for more than a few days. Have you seen these folk?

Once you pray for them and ask, "How do you feel?" they quickly respond with, "I feel so much better. Thank you for praying for me." Usually, the preacher feels good about their service to the Lord but has no idea that those people are so intent on disobeying the Lord in a particular area that they will be back at that altar in no time, begging for mercy and strength to keep going.

It's not that God is powerless to deliver them or that God lacks wisdom in convincing them to follow by faith; that is not the problem. The real issue is that disobedience is at the core, and they use all the shouting to hide it. Initially, the Philistines' camp panicked because of all the shouting, but the louder they got, the more the enemy began to wonder, Are these people for real? You see, the enemy had already heard about the signs and wonders that occurred when the Ark of the Covenant was among the Israelites. The Philistines started to fear because of the spiritual pep rally the Israelites were holding. They began to take stock of all that the Lord had done for Israel and said, **"Woe to us!"**

Yet somehow, the Philistines gained some courage and decided to fight against the Israelites, not wanting to become servants of the Hebrews, and they conducted themselves as brave men and fought.

When God Is Not On Your Side!

"So the Philistines fought, and Israel was defeated, and every man fled to his tent. There was a very great slaughter, and there fell of Israel thirty thousand foot soldiers. Also the ark of God was captured; and the two sons of Eli, Hophni and Phinehas, died."

To the dismay of the Philistines, they plundered the Hebrew children and slaughtered thirty thousand foot soldiers. Imagine that! Not only did they kill the soldiers, but they also captured the ark of God, and they killed the priest and his sons as well.

Nothing can hide disobedience. Not props! Not shouting! Not the number of soldiers! When God is against us because of our disobedience, the only thing that will save us is repentance for our sin of disobedience.

If we truly repent from the heart, the Lord will be on our side, and victory will be a sure guarantee. His favor will overtake us, and we will see His glory once again! Neh'enah.

47

The Discipline of Early!

"O God, You are my God;
Early will I seek You;
My soul thirsts for You;
My flesh longs for You
In a dry and thirsty land
Where there is no water." (Psalm 63:1)

In this wonderful prayer by King David, I discover some principles that can make our prayers powerful and life-changing.

Let me share my thoughts on this devotion: I believe God will speak to us as we seek to know Him more deeply and cultivate a more intimate relationship with Him.

Acknowledging Him!

Nothing is more powerful than exalting and recognizing our God as OUR God. To personalize our prayers by acknowledging our heavenly Father sends signals not only to our innermost being but also to every power and principality that might surround us.

Think about this. The very second that this prayer leaves your heart through your mouth, all hell knows where you stand!

Often, believers focus more on making their petitions known first than on acknowledging God's true nature. In their hearts, they are saying, I know you are there, God, but please hear my cry. I need you to do a miracle for me now!

As we learn to recognize God as our primary focus, we will develop a wonderful relationship with the living God. Nothing is purer than having this personal connection with the King of the universe!

The Discipline of *Early*!

Seeking God early is about more than just a specific time on the clock. It reflects the cultivation and growth of a relationship. When you love someone, all you want to do is spend your time with them. This is true in any relationship built on love.

When I met my wife, we would go on dates, and time would fly by so quickly that I would drop her off at her house by no later than midnight. I couldn't wait to see her again. This is how our relationship with Jesus should be!

In addition to the meaning of 'early,' it also conveys discipline. Jesus must be the first person you say good morning to. As soon as our eyes open, the first Person we see should be Jesus!

The Discipline of Early is not just words; it's an action. Those who seek Jesus early don't talk about it, they do it! It shows loyalty, commitment, and desire.

Thirsting & Longing!

King David expressed his heart in his prayer as he said, **"My soul thirsts for You; My flesh longs for You."**

What makes a man cry out for God in this manner? What makes a man say, I am thirsty for You?

The only thing that I believe makes a man so eager for God and longing for more is if that man has tasted the Lord's goodness. You can only feel these emotions burning in your spirit through revelation by the Holy Spirit.

A Land with No Water!

Being attuned to the flow of God and recognizing when the river of God has dried up in your soul is one of the keys to revival in anyone's heart. Too many believers are unaware of this. Either pride has taken root in their hearts or they are completely spiritually disconnected from the manifested presence of God in their lives.

Let us not delay in meeting God early! Every servant of God who has tasted the Lord's goodness knows well the value of seeking Him early. Let us rather lose sleep than skip prayer!

Early Morning Prayer

As I conclude my devotion, let me say that we, as believers, must learn the secret of knowing God. For those who hunger after righteousness, there is only one way to enter — it's through early morning prayer! Why early morning prayer?

Early morning prayer will bring you before God to start the day; yes, the day that the Lord has made for you to manifest His presence and glory wherever you go!

As you wake in the early morning hours, your mind and body are fresh and ready to receive. This provides an excellent foundation for the Lord to fill your life with every good thing, not to mention prophetic revelation from the Holy Spirit. Your needs, pain, struggles, fears, and doubts are alleviated when you come before God in complete humility and brokenness as well.

I choose early mornings to meet God mostly... I need to meet Him early!

My heart desires this more than anything. Ministry is what I do, but early mornings with God define who I am!

When this life finally comes to an end, people will remember us for the many things we did. Some will be admirable, while others might be shameful or embarrassing; however, when everything is said and done, I want to be known as a man who knew God! It is my hope that all my living and dying will bring glory to Jesus, my Lord! Neh'enah.

48

The Religious Spirit! – Part 1

"The Pharisee took his stand ostentatiously and began to pray thus before and with himself: God, I thank You that I am not like the rest of men—extortioners (robbers), swindlers [unrighteous in heart and life], adulterers—or even like this tax collector here. I fast twice a week; I give tithes of all that I gain." (Luke 18:11, 12 Amplified Version)

Here's a topic I've been pondering during my quiet times: The Religious Spirit. Have you ever heard of the religious spirit? Many in charismatic circles have frequently taught about this subject — the presence of this particular spirit moving within the hearts of God's people.

I believe that a religious spirit is more about the attitude of the heart than an actual entity causing havoc or possessing people. Although many have turned this religious spirit into a stronghold in people's lives, I still believe it is simply a person's heart failing to submit to the will of the Father!

I have been in meetings where it never fails that a preacher will say, You have a religious spirit in you! What does this mean, exactly? Are they making these claims because of the way the person dresses, speaks, thinks, acts, or the way they see God or the Scriptures?

What is this religious spirit that people are calling out?

A Mistaken Identity

Too often, those who call out this religious spirit are people who recognize the holiness of Christ in others. They see that these religious fanatics are practicing sound doctrine and following Christ. They know the commitment they have to the Lord, and it makes them feel uneasy; all they can do is say, 'They have a religious spirit!'

Now, I also realize that some believers can't help but boast about their faith and share with everyone the numerous revelations they receive from God, all the Scriptures they've memorized, or how many souls they've led to Christ in the past 24 hours. While doing something for God is admirable, those who brag are simply immature; I doubt they are influenced by this so-called religious spirit.

Iron Sharpens Iron!

Throughout my years of seeking God, I've noticed that those who are quick to accuse others of having a religious spirit are often guilty of it themselves. These servants tend to neglect obedience to God's laws, sound doctrine, and cultivating God's presence in their private lives. They are not willing to give their lives fully to follow the Lord with complete devotion.

So, it always seems that in trying to cover their nakedness, they are accusing someone else of the very same thing.

As for the religious spirit, I do believe it exists; I don't believe it is what people make it out to be. The simple fact that someone has an immature view of God and the Scripture is not a religious spirit; it's called immaturity!

As I mentioned before, a religious spirit is more an attitude of the heart than an entity waiting to trap Christians.

Practicing Maturity!

"Keep a close watch on yourself and on the teaching. Persist in this, for by so doing you will save both yourself and your hearers." (1 Timothy

4:16. ESV)

Let me share with you some principles that God's servants must practice, which some may mistakenly interpret as having a religious spirit.

In the Scripture above, the Apostle Paul tells the young Timothy to **"keep a watch on himself..."** This means watching his walk before God carefully, because others are following him. Also, he should ensure that he follows pure doctrine [teaching], not every wind of doctrine that comes and goes like a fad. The Apostle Paul concludes this message by saying, **"Persist in this!"**

For those applying 1 Timothy 4:16, know that you are part of a minority in this society. People who live loosely, compromise with the world, and have lukewarm lifestyles could label you as having a religious spirit these days.

Hold on Tight to Your Traditions! (Sound Doctrine)

"So then, brothers and sisters, stand firm and hold [tightly] to the traditions which you were taught, whether by word of mouth or by letter from us." (2 Thessalonians 2:15. Amplified Version)

Recalling a conversation with my spiritual mentor and pastor years ago, we talked about recent trends in Christianity—teachings that lack a true biblical foundation or are man-made efforts to satisfy the itching ears of the flesh.

As we talked, he told me this: David, people want to talk to me about new things and that God is doing a new thing, etc. But I want you to know that I am still shouting about the old stuff: the blood and the cross of Christ. I never forgot that. His words brought me great comfort as a young and emerging pastor.

As I conclude this first part of The Religious Spirit, let me reiterate this thought: Don't confuse a pursuit of God's holiness with a religious spirit. Neh'enah.

49

The Religious Spirit! – Part 2

"Two men went up into the temple to pray, one a Pharisee and the other a tax collector. The Pharisee, standing by himself, prayed thus: 'God, I thank you that I am not like other men, extortioners, unjust, adulterers, or even like this tax collector. I fast twice a week; I give tithes of all that I get.' But the tax collector, standing far off, would not even lift up his eyes to heaven, but beat his breast, saying, 'God, be merciful to me, a sinner!' I tell you, this man went down to his house justified, rather than the other. For everyone who exalts himself will be humbled, but the one who humbles himself will be exalted." (Luke 18:10-14 ESV)

To better understand the religious spirit, let us look at the story mentioned above as told by Jesus himself.

When addressing the so-called religious spirit, we must look beyond the façade people put up when they speak. We need to look past the dress code, actions, and boasting.

A Religious Spirit Or Downright Pride?

In our previous text, you will notice it speaks of two men who went to the temple to pray. It involved two human beings with two different labels. One was a Pharisee by religion; the other was a tax collector by occupation (usually tax collectors were known for their abuse of power and how they stole from taxpayers).

They both approached God and made their requests: The Pharisee went first and stood alone. What does this reveal about the man? It shows that he considered himself too holy and self-righteous to be near anyone who didn't share his religious practices.

'God, I Thank You That I Am Not Like Other Men!

The Pharisee started to pray and said, 'God, I thank you that I am not like other men, extortioners, unjust, adulterers, or even like this tax collector. I fast twice a week; I give tithes of all that I get.'

I don't know about you, but immediately from the start, this Pharisee brings God into his mess! He says, **"God, I thank you that I am not like other men!"** What does this mean? It means that the Pharisee is cornering God by thanking him that he was not made like the loser tax collector! Do you see this?

Did this Pharisee have a religious spirit? Not! He had a bad case of pure old-fashioned pride! To say that this man had a religious spirit controlling him would be to take the responsibility away from the Pharisee for his fleshly display of pride. In plain, the Pharisee was so full of himself! Do you agree?

The Pharisee continues to mention in his prayer to God how he is not only different from the tax collector but also better than him! I think he was praying out loud and assuming that this tax collector was probably into extortion, injustice, and adultery.

He ends his prayer by reaffirming his commitment to his Pharisaic practices, including fasting twice a week and giving his tithes.

Would we call this a religious spirit? Is this immaturity on behalf of this Pharisee? Or is it downright pride? I believe it's pride!

A Basic Display of Humility!

But the tax collector, standing far off, would not even lift up his eyes to heaven, but beat his breast, saying, **'God, be merciful to me, a sinner!'**

If you've ever struggled against sin and fought to find victory, then you would understand the tax collector's prayer.

Now, if you have never accepted your weaknesses and have always exalted yourself above those who have embraced their fallen nature and learned to rely on God's grace and mercy for survival, then you would understand what a repentant heart before God looks like.

The tax collector wasn't trying to sound spiritual; he wasn't trying to portray himself as self-righteous, and he wasn't trying to look good in front of those who could hear him pray (mainly the Pharisee next to him). He was simply trying to touch the hem of God's garment and find rest for his soul. He wasn't listing his spiritual accomplishments; no sir, he was 'standing far off, would not even lift up his eyes to heaven, but beat his breast, saying, 'God, be merciful to me, a sinner!'

Jesus Takes Note!

"For everyone who exalts himself will be humbled, but the one who humbles himself will be exalted."

Jesus said that the tax collector went home justified by the way he displayed his heart before God.

After this, Christ continued to say that anyone who exalts themselves will be humbled, but the one who humbles themselves will be exalted.

As you can see, there is no religious spirit present. If there were, Jesus would have shown better discernment. He missed it! Or perhaps Jesus understood the human heart well enough to realize that what was in that

Pharisee's heart and life wasn't a genuine religious spirit, but outright pride! Neh'enah.

50

How Will I Serve Him?

"Now it happened as they went that He entered a certain village; and a certain woman named Martha welcomed Him into her house. And she had a sister called Mary, who also sat at Jesus' feet and heard His word. But Martha was distracted with much serving, and she approached Him and said, "Lord, do You not care that my sister has left me to serve alone? Therefore tell her to help me." And Jesus answered and said to her, "Martha, Martha, you are worried and troubled about many things. But one thing is needed, and Mary has chosen that good part, which will not be taken away from her." (Luke 10:38-42)

This morning, the Holy Spirit opened my understanding to see some things in the Scriptures that, in my opinion, lay a foundation for intimacy and service to God.

Intimacy and service unto Him are the two things Jesus highlighted in Mark 12:28-32: "Then one of the scribes came, and having heard them reasoning together, perceiving that He had answered them well, asked Him, "Which is the first commandment of all?" Jesus answered him, "The first of all the commandments is: 'Hear, O Israel, the LORD our God, the LORD is one. And you shall love the LORD your God with all your heart, with all your soul, with all your mind, and with all your strength.' This is the first commandment. And the second, like it, is this: 'You shall love your neighbor as yourself.' There is no other commandment greater than these."

In the book of Luke, we see the two sisters Martha and Mary welcoming Jesus into their home. At first, this seems like a normal visit, but there was clearly something very profound that Jesus was about to reveal.

It's always a good thing to know that if Jesus visits us, it is with intention. Ask yourself: What is He doing at my house?

Two Types of Servants

The Scripture notes that the two sisters welcomed Jesus into their home; however, they had different personalities. One sister, named Mary, wanted to sit at Jesus' feet and listen to His words. The other sister, named Martha, was "distracted" with much serving.

Let me delve a bit deeper into this distraction. The Scripture says that Martha was **"distracted with much serving."** The original Greek word for distracted means *to pull away or to draw away*.

Martha was being pulled away from what was most important, which was to sit at the feet of Jesus and listen to His words. Was Martha in the wrong? When is serving considered wrong?

I believe serving is wrong when someone does it with selfish or incorrect motives, like seeking affirmation, acceptance, or recognition. It's wrong when serving is done with the goal of pleasing people.

Now, please understand my point of view: serving God is what we are called to do. When we do it, we should consider what kind of heart we have and what purpose we have in mind. These questions must be answered before doing anything for Jesus!

Now, I believe both are necessary. We must welcome Jesus, but we also need to prepare the meal we are serving. So, the question arises: Does He feed us spiritual food, or do we feed Him natural food? Or do we partake of both?

We Do Both!

True service to the Lord is performed intentionally once we understand what He is asking us to do for Him.

True service is born in God's heart and then shared with ours. What we do with the information depends on our faith to believe and our willingness to obey wherever He leads.

Many years ago, at a Street Minister's Conference held in Dallas, Texas, which I attended, I heard David Wilkeson speak on prayer and how it was the secret to a successful life in God. In his message, he stated: *"All ministry must come out of communion with God."* Since then, I have made this my motto for everything I do in Jesus' name.

When we wait for God to speak to us and guide us with His eye, our ministry will carry God's anointing and authority. One can do many things in Jesus' Name, but did Jesus instruct us to do them?

Always remember that a good servant waits for his master's wishes to be revealed, then runs as fast as he can to carry them out.

As Jesus entered Martha and Mary's house, they should have both set aside everything they were doing and sat with Jesus to listen to His heart. This should be our primary calling – to sit at His feet. Not to try impressing Him with our good works, projects, or achievements. Let us sit at His feet and wait for divine revelation! Neh'enah.

51

Have I Lost My Passion for Jesus?

What is passion? How can we define it? Passion is an emotion; it's an intense, driving, or overpowering feeling or conviction. It's also an ardent affection: love. It involves a strong liking, desire, or devotion to some activity, object, or concept.

As I studied and prayed over this searing devotion, I couldn't help but ask some questions that I believe will give us a fair evaluation of where we stand with Jesus today.

Apart from having a genuine encounter with His presence and an overwhelming experience with the Person of the Holy Spirit, how can it be that people tend to slowly drift away from where Christ has placed them?

You see, He took us out of a life of sin and compromise; a life where we were destitute and separated from God in this world. He shed His blood on Calvary's cross and then died, but rose again on the third day—never to die again! This same Jesus invited you into this life and made it available to us so that we might believe and accept it.

Now, don't get me wrong, some people are very grateful to have been rescued and delivered from such a terrible life, and their testimony reflects that. However, others have experienced the life of God, but as they began to grow in the Lord, the demands to follow Him increased; yes, the expectations started to become clearer, and they no longer felt as happy about it.

Only Half-Way?

"Then Jesus said to them, "Most assuredly, I say to you, unless you eat the flesh of the Son of Man and drink His blood, you have no life in you. Whoever eats My flesh and drinks My blood has eternal life, and I will raise him up at the last day. For My flesh is food indeed, and My blood is drink indeed. He who eats My flesh and drinks My blood abides in Me, and I in him. As the living Father sent Me, and I live because of the Father, so he who feeds on Me will live because of Me. This is the bread which came down from heaven—not as your fathers ate the manna, and are dead. He who eats this bread will live forever." These things He said in the synagogue as He taught in Capernaum.

Therefore many of His disciples, when they heard this, said, "This is a hard saying; who can understand it?"

When Jesus knew in Himself that His disciples complained about this, He said to them, "Does this offend you? What then if you should see the Son of Man ascend where He was before? It is the Spirit who gives life; the flesh profits nothing. The words that I speak to you are spirit, and they are life. But there are some of you who do not believe." For Jesus knew from the beginning who they were who did not believe, and who would betray Him. And He said, "Therefore I have said to you that no one can come to Me unless it has been granted to him by My Father." From that time many of His disciples went back and walked with Him no more." (John 6:53-66)

In sharing this powerful message that Jesus gave to those who followed Him, mainly His disciples, He began describing a walk that required commitment and carried high expectations. Unless the Spirit of God guided them along that path, they wouldn't be able to follow. It was that simple.

Was Jesus trying to be mean? How about insensitive? Was He trying to scare people away from His kingdom?

Though it may appear from first glance that He was being insensitive to those poor and hungry followers, He wasn't! Jesus was bringing the revelation to the table – the revelation that would be needed to endure the race.

He wasn't concerned about masses of people following; He wasn't concerned about giving favor to His people just because they had been following for days now. No, Jesus was trying to teach those following that one must enter His life so that He may enter theirs, if they were going to survive this wicked world. These needed to take place if they were to receive revelation from the Father.

Will the next spiritual lesson in your life discourage you? Will the next temptation sidetrack you? Will the next wave of critics make you quit on Jesus?

There are many lessons to learn yet; don't be shaken by the things you are presently suffering. Jesus only wants to know if you are still in love with Him and are willing to follow Him wherever He goes. Neh'enah.

52

Called to be An Expression of His Nature!

"You are the light of the world. A city that is set on a hill cannot be hidden. Nor do they light a lamp and put it under a basket, but on a lampstand, and it gives light to all who are in the house. Let your light so shine before men, that they may see your good works and glorify your Father in heaven." (Matthew 5:14-16)

A few weeks ago, God revealed His heart to me in a way I hadn't experienced before. He first opened my natural eyes and then granted me spiritual insight into the needs of others.

My wife and I headed into a local hamburger spot to grab an early dinner on a Sunday afternoon. The place was crowded as usual, but we managed to find a table amid the chaos, thank goodness!

As I looked at the long line where we ordered, I noticed an older lady going from table to table. It seemed that she was trying to sell some merchandise she had in her pocket. When I looked closer, I saw she was selling keychains. They were lovely keychains with the Virgin Mary's emblem imprinted on them. I am not a fan of keychains, and I am especially not a worshipper of the Virgin Mary (since religions often use her as a lucky charm).

As we lined up and moved forward to place our order, I asked the young lady taking our order, "Do you guys give food to the hungry? Do you provide meals for anyone in need?" She looked at me a bit puzzled and finally said, "I don't believe so, sir." She then asked me why I was asking. I said, There is a lady in your dining area who is asking for money for food."

God's Test

After we placed our order and sat down, I kept looking at the lady who was making her rounds; it seemed no one had bought anything from her, but she kept trying to make a sale with perseverance.

Finally, the lady reached our table, placed all her keychains on top of it, and began to show us the crafts. As she displayed the different keychains, I stopped her and asked, Are you selling these items so you can get money to eat? She replied, Yes. I am hungry and no one is buying. My heart was moved with compassion, and I could almost hear God saying, *What are you going to do about this, David?*

Without hesitation, I stood up from my table and told the lady to come with me, saying we were going to get her a delicious meal. She came next to me, and we joined the line. The girl who had helped me before was there again. I said to the worker, Please take this lady's order. Whatever she wants, it doesn't matter the cost. I am paying for her meal. She replied, Okay, sir. The lady ordered a big meal and enjoyed it.

The Real Joy Comes in Giving!

No one knows how much my heart rejoiced in serving this lady. My meal was delicious, but the joy in my heart was overwhelming. I didn't do it for others to notice, to feel good about myself, or to earn points in heaven. I did it because that's what I would want someone to do for me if I were in that situation. Plus, twenty dollars is a better investment for God than just staying in my pocket!

As I reflected that afternoon after I got home, I started to think about how many people in that restaurant could have helped this lady, but no one did. I asked the Lord, *'Why did you choose me, Lord, to do this?'* He said, *'I knew I could trust you, David.'*

Can We Be Trusted With an Increase?

So, this leads me to ask: Can God trust us with anything, like a promotion? When you get a small break at work and a long-awaited raise, how will you thank God beyond your personal tithes? Or maybe you did so well last quarter and received a generous bonus; what part of it did you give to the hungry, the naked, or the poor?

What about giving a generous gift to the missionary who is bringing the gospel to other parts of the world—yes, those areas where you and I will probably never go? We must live with the understanding that our lives should reflect His nature wherever we are. We must escape from the ideology that says, It is all about me, me, me!

The nature of Jesus and those who truly love God is that of cheerful givers. Our God is a giving God, and what better way to be a light to the world than through the expression of love done in the name of Jesus? Neh'enah.

For more books written by David Mayorga, please visit:

www.shabarpublications.com

www.ingramcontent.com/pod-product-compliance
Lightning Source LLC
Chambersburg PA
CBHW030243010526
44107CB00030B/1322/J